The Heart *of* It's a Wonderful Life

*How the Most Inspirational Movie
of All Time Still Inspires the Spirit*

JIMMY HAWKINS

HARPER HORIZON

The Heart of It's a Wonderful Life

Copyright © 2025 by The Jimmy Hawkins Co.

All rights reserved. No portion of this book may be reproduced, stored in a retrieval system, or transmitted in any form or by any means—electronic, mechanical, photocopy, recording, scanning, or other—except for brief quotations in critical reviews or articles, without the prior written permission of the publisher.

Published by Harper Horizon, an imprint of HarperCollins Focus LLC, 501 Nelson Place, Nashville, TN 37214, USA.

It's a Wonderful Life is a trademark owned by Republic Entertainment Inc.®, a subsidiary of Spelling Entertainment Group Inc.® Republic Entertainment Inc. has not approved or endorsed this publication.

Unless otherwise noted, Scripture quotations are taken from the Holy Bible, New International Version®, NIV®. Copyright © 1973, 1978, 1984, 2011 by Biblica, Inc.® Used by permission of Zondervan. All rights reserved worldwide. www.zondervan.com. The "NIV" and "New International Version" are trademarks registered in the United States Patent and Trademark Office by Biblica, Inc.®

Scripture quotations marked MSG are taken from The Message. Copyright © 1993, 2002, 2018 by Eugene H. Peterson. Used by permission of NavPress. All rights reserved. Represented by Tyndale House Publishers, Inc.

Any internet addresses, phone numbers, or company or product information printed in this book are offered as a resource and are not intended in any way to be or to imply an endorsement by Harper Horizon, nor does Harper Horizon vouch for the existence, content, or services of these sites, phone numbers, companies, or products beyond the life of this book.

ISBN 978-1-4002-5512-2 (ePub)
ISBN 978-1-4002-5510-8 (HC)

Without limiting the exclusive rights of any author, contributor or the publisher of this publication, any unauthorized use of this publication to train generative artificial intelligence (AI) technologies is expressly prohibited. HarperCollins also exercise their rights under Article 4(3) of the Digital Single Market Directive 2019/790 and expressly reserve this publication from the text and data mining exception.

HarperCollins Publishers, Macken House, 39/40 Mayor Street Upper, Dublin 1, D01 C9W8, Ireland (https://www.harpercollins.com)

Library of Congress Control Number: 2025938471

Art direction: Belinda Bass
Cover Design: Gearbox Design Studio
Interior Design: Denise Froehlich

Printed in the United States of America

25 26 27 28 29 LBC 5 4 3 2 1

Dedicated to the cast and crew of *It's a Wonderful Life*

The cast and crew of It's a Wonderful Life *at a wrap picnic hosted by Frank Capra and Jimmy Stewart, August 4, 1946.*

Contents

From the Author..vii
Introduction.. ix

SCENE 1	CAPRAVISION.....................................1
SCENE 2	AN ANSWER TO OUR PRAYERS 11
SCENE 3	THE HERO INSIDE OF YOU 15
SCENE 4	FOLLOW YOUR DREAMS.........................23
SCENE 5	TRUST YOUR INSTINCT 29
SCENE 6	NO REGRETS...................................35
SCENE 7	DANCE BY THE LIGHT OF THE MOON 43
SCENE 8	STUCK IN BEDFORD FALLS...................... 49
SCENE 9	LASSO THE MOON...............................61
SCENE 10	A RUN ON THE BANK 69
SCENE 11	WELCOME TO BAILEY PARK......................79
SCENE 12	THAT'S MY BUSINESS. BUILDING AND LOAN 85
SCENE 13	WHERE'S THE MONEY? 93
SCENE 14	WHAT'S THE MATTER WITH DADDY?............. 99
SCENE 15	YOU'RE WORTH MORE DEAD THAN ALIVE........111

SCENE 16	"I'M NOT A PRAYING MAN, BUT..."	123
SCENE 17	YOU REALLY HAD A WONDERFUL LIFE. DON'T YOU SEE?	131
SCENE 18	"I WANT TO LIVE AGAIN"	147
SCENE 19	NO MAN IS A FAILURE WHO HAS FRIENDS	155

Conclusion: After All Is Said and Done 169
Epilogue 173
Acknowledgments 177
Notes 178
About the Author 182

From the Author

My name is Jimmy Hawkins. I played Jimmy Stewart and Donna Reed's youngest son, Tommy Bailey, in the Frank Capra holiday classic *It's a Wonderful Life*.

The heart of *It's a Wonderful Life* is the profound message that every individual's life has a significant impact on the world, even if it seems insignificant. George Bailey's revelation, shown through Clarence's intervention, underscores the interconnectedness of human lives and the ripple effect of our actions. The film highlights how George's life, seemingly ordinary, touched countless others in Bedford Falls, impacting their well-being, their relationships, and the overall community.

This book was written to share with you many unpublished facts I've collected about cast and crew these past ten years. They all were kind enough to share their relatives' personal stories, family photos, and 8-mm home movies, giving us a clearer understanding of what they brought to the scripted pages. You'll

FROM THE AUTHOR

realize scene by scene what makes us so emotionally moved by this life-changing film and why the heart of *It's a Wonderful Life* still inspires the spirit.

Jimmy Hawkins

Introduction

It's a Wonderful Life *isn't the way life is . . .
just the way it should be!*

—FRANK CAPRA

My admiration for Frank Capra runs deep. His vision for *It's a Wonderful Life* and his insistence on driving its themes home time and again was my North Star as I wrote this book, so let's start by hearing from Frank himself—the visionary responsible for making *It's a Wonderful Life*, voted the most inspirational movie of all time by the American Film Institute.

> I didn't give a film-clip whether critics hailed or hooted *Wonderful Life*. I thought it was the greatest film I had ever made. Better yet, I thought it was the greatest film *anybody* ever made. It wasn't made for the oh-so-bored critics, or the oh-so jaded literati. It was my kind of film for my kind of people; the motion picture I wanted to make since I first peered into a movie camera's eyepiece....
>
> A film to tell the weary, the disheartened, and the disillusioned; the wino, the junkie, the prostitute: those behind prison walls and those behind Iron Curtains, that *no man is a failure*!
>
> To show those born slow of foot or slow of mind, those oldest sisters condemned to spinsterhood, and those oldest sons condemned to unschooled toil, that *each man's life touches so*

many other lives. And that if he isn't around it would leave an awful hole.

A film that said to the downtrodden, the pushed around, the pauper, "Heads up, fella. No man is poor who has one friend. Three friends and you're filthy rich."

A film that expressed its love for the homeless and the loveless; for her for whose cross is heavy and him whose touch is ashes; for the Magdalenes stoned by hypocrites and the afflicted Lazaruses with only dogs to lick their sores.

I wanted to shout to the abandoned grandfathers staring vacantly in nursing homes, to the always-interviewed but seldom-adopted half-breed orphans, to the paupers who refuse to die while medical vultures wait to snatch their hearts and livers, and to those who take cobalt treatments and whistle—I wanted to shout, "You are the salt of the earth. And *It's a Wonderful Life* is my memorial to you!"

In the Beginning . . .

On the morning of February 12, 1938, American writer Philip Van Doren Stern had an idea while shaving. When he finished shaving, he wrote down a two-page treatment about a man who wishes he had never been born. He set it aside. From time to time he shared it with friends, who encouraged him to write more. When he added a Christmas theme, it just seemed right. He sent it out to various magazines and publishers but received

INTRODUCTION

only rejections. Yet he didn't give up. He still had heart for his story.

Stern privately published it and sent it out to two hundred friends as a Christmas card. One friend was his Hollywood agent, Shirley Collier. After reading it she called and told him she thought the story had the makings of a movie.

In 1943 RKO bought the rights for $10,000. Philip Van Doren Stern never gave up. If he had, there would have never been an *It's a Wonderful Life*.

Even the origin of what became *It's a Wonderful Life*—this short story that continued to tug at its author's heart—is such a story of perseverance. Stern couldn't set the idea aside and went so far as to publish it himself so he could share it. Imagine if he hadn't persisted. The world would have missed out on something so special.

And it's a lesson for us too—if you have a dream, you can't give up!

Once RKO had purchased the story, their goal was to tailor the script to be a vehicle for movie star Cary Grant. They hired three of Hollywood's finest screenwriters and their teams to begin adapting the story into a script. First was Dalton Trumbo. His script ended up being political—George was "a politician who rises from an idealistic state assemblyman to a cynical congressman, contemptuous of the people he represents." When that script failed, they brought in screenwriters Marc Connelly and Clifford Odets. But none of the three scripts worked for the studio. In 1945, RKO made a distribution deal with Academy Award–winning director Frank Capra and his newly established Liberty Films production company.

Capra had just been discharged from the army and hadn't looked through a camera's eye in the four years he spent in World War II. One night, the wife of RKO's studio chief, Charles Koerner, suggested that Capra would be perfect for that Christmas card project. Koerner agreed. Again, someone didn't give up. (See, that's you. Don't give up!)

The next day, Koerner personally presented *The Greatest Gift* to Capra and told him he could have Van Doren Stern's card and the three failed screenplays for $50,000—what they had invested in the project thus far. That night Capra read everything. He didn't think the screenplays captured what was in the card, but he felt it was the greatest idea he had ever heard: A man gets to see what life would have been like if he had never been born. Capra purchased it and hired Frances Goodrich and Albert Hackett to adapt it.

They retitled the story *It's a Wonderful Life*.

And bingo!

Capra had his first postwar movie.

INTRODUCTION

"The Greatest Gift," The Capra Way

You're likely already familiar with the plot of *It's a Wonderful Life*, but in case you need a refresher, here's how Frank Capra shaped it into the film we know and love today. The film's brilliant technique of flashbacks tells this story in such a powerful way.

Bedford Falls, where It's a Wonderful Life *takes place.*

1946, CHRISTMAS EVE

George Bailey, played by Jimmy Stewart, is standing at the edge of a tall bridge. He is suicidal. Clarence Oddbody, played by Henry Travers, an AS2 (Angel Second Class), has been sent down to earth by the head angel, Joseph, to save George. If Clarence completes this mission, he'll earn his wings—an achievement he's been working toward for more than two hundred years. But first, Clarence must get to know George Bailey.

INTRODUCTION

1919

It's 1919, and young George Bailey, played by Bobby Anderson, is twelve years old. George saves the life of his younger brother, Harry (Georgie Nokes), after a horrible accident causes Harry to fall through the ice and into the frigid waters of the frozen pond they're sledding on. After this save, George catches a cold that ends up settling in his left ear and damaging his hearing.

George spends three weeks recovering from that harrowing incident before he's able to return to his job as the errand boy at Gower Drugs. It's here that we meet a young Violet Bick (Jeanine Anne Roose) and Mary Hatch (Jeanne Gail). Violet is a flirt—she likes all the boys, including George. But young Mary only has eyes for George. George tells the girls he wants to travel and see the world.

During this time, George prevents his boss, the pharmacist Mr. Gower (H. B. Warner), from accidentally filling a child's prescription with poison. Mr. Gower, grief-stricken over the death of his son from influenza, had begun to drink, which led to the deadly prescription. George stops the poisoned pills from being delivered just in time to both save the child and to save Mr. Gower from jail and disgrace.

By 1928, George has saved enough money to go to college and make that trip to "see the world."

He goes to buy a piece of luggage. For a trip like this, it'll need to be a big suitcase—one that that will see a thousand nights and many miles. While at the store, he learns that his former

INTRODUCTION

boss, Mr. Gower, had come in and purchased a suitcase for him. George goes to Gower Drugs to thank him. When he leaves, he runs into Bert (Ward Bond) and Ernie (Frank Faylen), George's best friends.

That night, George is home with his dad, Pa Bailey (Samuel S. Hinds), having his last dinner at the old Bailey Boarding House. Tomorrow he leaves on his trip to see the world. George and his dad talk about George's dreams and why he can't take his pop's place at Bailey Brothers Building and Loan.

There is commotion in the background as younger brother Harry (Todd Karns) is getting ready to leave for his graduation night.

His pop tells him, "No gin tonight, son."

"Aw, Pop, just a little?" Harry presses.

"No, son, not one drop."

After a long-overdue intimate talk with his pop, George says, "I think I'll get dressed and go over to Harry's party."

Pop says, "Have a good time, son."

At Harry's high school grad night (class of 1928), George runs into longtime friends Sam "Hee-Haw" Wainwright (Frank Albertson) and Marty Hatch (Harold Landon).

Marty tells George that his sister Mary (Donna Reed) is there.

"Be a sport, just dance with her one time," Marty says, "and you'll give her the thrill of her life."

George and Mary end up in the big dance contest and eventually in the swimming pool.

INTRODUCTION

As he walks her home, George discusses his future with Mary. They stop and talk about the old run-down Granville house at 320 Sycamore. Seems if you make a wish throwing a rock at the old place and break a window, your wish will come true. Mary does.

They're interrupted when Harry and the boys' uncle Billy (Thomas Mitchell) drive up and tell George that his father has had a stroke and to get home right away.

George and Harry's father dies that night.

At a board meeting after the funeral, Old Man Potter (Lionel Barrymore), a greedy member of the board of directors for the Building and Loan, tries to gain control of the institution. George talks the board into stopping Potter's takeover; they agree, but only on the condition that George run the business. George reluctantly stays in Bedford Falls and gives his college money to his brother, with the idea that Harry will take over the business once he finishes his education.

1932, Four Years Later

George is excited for Harry's return from college, as Harry is supposed to take over the Building and Loan. George's hopes of leaving Bedford Falls are again dashed when Harry announces he has gotten married and his wife's father has offered Harry a job he can't refuse in another town. George cannot bring himself to ruin his brother's prospects.

There is a wedding announcement party at the Baileys' house, with family and close friends like Bert and Ernie. George

INTRODUCTION

has a lot on his mind, so he takes a walk. He runs into grown-up Violet (Gloria Grahame), who has become quite a looker. George ends up at Mary Hatch's house. While there, Sam Wainwright calls. Sam, now very successful, had always been attracted to Mary (and every other girl he met). During the phone call, George, reluctantly at first, confesses his love to Mary and they share a passionate first kiss.

George and Mary eventually get married. On their wedding day, there is a run on the bank. The Building and Loan almost goes under until Mary offers the couple's honeymoon money ($2,000) to save it.

Later, Mary and George put a down payment on the old Granville house at 320 Sycamore. It means so much to Mary. She and George made wishes on it when they first dated. Mary confides to George that this was her wish when she broke the window.

George only wanted to be an architect and build things. He was designing all the time to be ready when he left Bedford Falls to see the world. He designs and builds Bailey Park, an affordable-housing project. The first homeowner is bar owner Martini and his family. They and the other town residents are rescued from paying high rents in the slums of Old Man Potter.

Potter grouses to his property manager that the Bailey Park homes "are worth twice what they cost to build."

Devious Potter tempts George with a job paying him almost ten times what he is making at the Building and Loan. Intrigued

── INTRODUCTION ──

at first, George realizes that Potter is trying to buy him off and walks out, calling Potter "a scurvy little spider."

1938–1946

Over the next several years, George and Mary raise a growing family.

The Bailey Family: George, Mary, Peter, Janie, Zuzu, and Tommy.

When World War II erupts, George is designated as 4-F because of his hearing loss, making him unfit to serve.

Harry, on the other hand, joins the navy and becomes a pilot. He is awarded the Congressional Medal of Honor for shooting down fifteen enemy aircraft, including two Japanese kamikaze planes that were about to crash into a navy troop transport.

INTRODUCTION

1946, CHRISTMAS EVE

On December 24, Uncle Billy encounters Mr. Potter while making a deposit in his bank. Bursting with pride, Billy shows him the front page of the *Bedford Falls Sentinel*. His nephew Harry is being honored by the president.

Absentmindedly, Uncle Billy leaves an envelope containing $8,000 in the folds of the newspaper. Potter discovers it later in his office and keeps it.

Beyond the money being missing looms a bigger problem: Bank examiners are in town to inspect the Building and Loan's records. When George learns of Billy's mistake, he comes undone, knowing that the bank examiner will soon discover the shortfall.

That night, George comes home and takes out his anger on Mary and the children: Peter (Larry Simms), Janie (Carol Coombs), Zuzu (Karolyn Grimes), and Tommy (Jimmy Hawkins—yeah, that's me!). Zuzu has caught a cold because she came home from school without a coat. George visits Zuzu's room upstairs and fixes the petals on the rose she was awarded at school. When he goes downstairs, his anger erupts, and he calls the teacher to yell about how irresponsible it was for her to send Zuzu home without her coat.

Then he starts in on his kids.

George has a little workspace off the living room where he designs miniature skyscrapers, bridges, and so on. Suddenly he starts kicking and smashing them all. He turns to see the shocked faces of his family. In frustration, he leaves. Mary is

INTRODUCTION

dumbfounded. George isn't like this. Something must be drastically wrong. Mary gets on the phone immediately.

In desperation, George visits Potter and tells him that he has misplaced the $8,000. He appeals to Potter for a loan to rescue the Bailey company.

Potter, knowing that Uncle Billy is actually the one who misplaced the money, reacts with feigned surprise to what George is saying. Potter turns George down: "You used to be so cocky. You called me a warped, frustrated old man. I'm going to swear out a warrant. The bank examiner is still here."

Soon afterward, George crashes his car into a tree during a snowstorm and runs to a nearby bridge. He contemplates suicide. Before he can leap, Clarence the Angel jumps into the water.

After George rescues him, Clarence reveals himself to be George's guardian angel and tries to help him. When George says he wishes he had never been born, Clarence grants George his wish: "Okay, you've never been born." Clarence now goes about showing him how life in Bedford Falls would have turned out if George had never existed.

In this version of reality, Bedford Falls is now Pottersville—a slum. Main Street is dominated by pawnshops, sleazy bars, and juke joints filled with dancers.

Bailey Park was never built; the land is now a cemetery. George's home, the old Granville house, remains run-down and abandoned.

On the street George greets people he knows, but in this

INTRODUCTION

"never been born" world, he doesn't exist, so they don't recognize him.

For George, Clarence's warning hasn't sunk in yet.

Mr. Gower, the pharmacist, was convicted of poisoning the child whose prescription George wasn't around to stop delivery of. Gower spent years in prison. Martini doesn't own the bar. Ernie and Bert are still friends, but they don't know George. Violet is an exotic dancer who is being arrested.

George isn't accepting what's going on.

Uncle Billy is in an insane asylum. Harry is dead; George wasn't around to save him when he fell through the ice. Consequently, Harry wasn't alive to serve in World War II and didn't save anyone on the transport.

In denial, George goes to his mother's house. She'll know him, he thinks, but she doesn't recognize him either. He leaves shaken and afraid.

He asks Clarence, "Where's Mary? She'll know me." But when they meet, she doesn't. George continues to reach out to her, but she screams and runs away. George is frantically looking for Clarence.

With nowhere to turn, George runs back to the bridge and leans against the railing. "Please, God, let me live again," he prays. "Let me live again."

His prayer is answered, and George is returned to the moment he met Clarence. George runs home, filled with a new appreciation for the meaning of his life. At the house, he finds his friends

---- INTRODUCTION ----

and family have collected a large laundry basket of money to save George and the Building and Loan.

Seeing those who have come to support him, George realizes how many people love him and how important he is to Bedford Falls. George's life—even if it wasn't what he expected—has meaning. Harry, who has flown in, proposes a toast: "To my big brother George, the richest man in town."

Amid the celebration, a bell tinkles on the Christmas tree.

Zuzu points to it and remarks, "Look, Daddy, Teacher says every time a bell rings, an angel gets his wings."

George smiles as he realizes that Clarence has finally earned his wings.

As the movie closes, we share George's epiphany: No matter what problems we have, it's a wonderful life.

SCENE 1

Capravision

I had found the story I had been looking for all my life . . . by light-years.

—FRANK CAPRA

At the time he began working on *It's a Wonderful Life*, Frank Capra likely would have been the last person in Hollywood to claim that there was anything wonderful about life. Capra, who had already directed successful classics such as *Mr. Deeds Goes to Town* and *Mr. Smith Goes to Washington*, was shocked to discover in the waning months of World War II that his former boss, Harry Cohn of Columbia (and possibly others), hadn't seemed to lament his absence from Hollywood while he was making army documentaries.

In the Hollywood that Capra was returning to postwar, studio heads wanted to control every part of making a movie. This simply didn't work for Capra, which is why he and his cohorts wanted to be independent. They wanted artistic control and not to be beholden to the will of execs.

By this point, Capra had already won three Academy Awards for Best Director, along with many other nominations and wins for his films, but making *It's a Wonderful Life* was like starting over again.

Hostility was brewing between Capra and the traditional studios due to disagreements related to marketing, lack of independence, and direction by committee. This tension prompted

Liberty Films partners (left to right) Frank Capra, William Wyler, George Stevens, and Samuel Briskin.

Capra to form a partnership with producer Samuel Briskin and, later, directors William Wyler and George Stevens, in an independent venture called Liberty Films.

As president of Liberty, Capra did not return to Hollywood with hat in hand. Rather, he threw down the gauntlet to the assembly line "committee system" used by other major studios such as Columbia, MGM, United Artists, Fox, Universal, and Paramount.

Already something of an outcast because of his conflicts with the major studios, Capra defied gossip columnist Hedda Hopper's reporting when he cast Donna Reed for the role of Mary Hatch instead of Ginger Rogers, as Hopper had proposed in her column.

When it came to developing the script, Capra continued to stick to his convictions. The writers who emerged with the major credit—Frances Goodrich and her husband, Albert Hackett—turned in some bright, sensitive scenes, but Capra still wasn't satisfied. He ended up writing some of the scenes himself. It wasn't a harmonious working relationship. It was especially frustrating for Goodrich and Hackett to learn that Capra was bringing on other writers to rewrite *while* they were still working on their draft, writers such as Dorothy Parker, Jo Swerling, and Michael Wilson. I think Wilson may have been brought in to work on the Potter character.

In the end, Capra had the script he wanted as well as screenwriting credit, alongside Goodrich and Hackett. It is said that when Goodrich and Hackett's invitation to the premiere arrived, they refused to see the completed picture because of what they described as their "horrid" experience with Capra.

Capra's conflicts with others continued as the filmmaking moved forward. During production, Capra and cinematographer Victor Milner (Oscar winner for Best Cinematography on Cecil B. DeMille's *Cleopatra*) crossed swords continually. Capra found the veteran cameraman "slow and pretentious."

Victor didn't care for some of what Capra was doing and one day made the mistake of telling Capra to leave the set until he was ready to shoot. That was the wrong way to talk to Capra!

Vic was replaced by Capra's longtime cameraman, Joseph Walker, and then again with Joseph Biroc when Walker had to return to Columbia to shoot another film due to a prior commitment.

Even during postproduction, Capra got into hairpulling with his music composer, Dimitri Tiomkin. Capra and Tiomkin had done five movies together, as well as a series of films during World War II. But on *It's a Wonderful Life*, Capra and Tiomkin weren't in sync. Capra claimed that Tiomkin was so absorbed with another score he was working on (for the Selznick western *Duel in the Sun*) that he had been giving *It's a Wonderful Life* only the leavings of his energies.

Although a collaborative work environment would be the ultimate goal, in many instances, Frank Capra's driving vision for the film led to conflict. But Capra knew what he wanted and did not deviate from that—even if it led to some challenges.

Frank Capra had an unswerving vision for *It's a Wonderful Life*. Nothing would deter him from bringing that vision to completion. We can learn a lot from that focus, including the importance of:

- Knowing what you want and going after it.
- Realizing that you can't borrow ambition. Achieving your ultimate goal is a do-it-yourself proposition all the way.
- Having a plan and setting that plan in motion. People

respect when a person has a clear vision and goes after what they want. They may not agree with the vision, but it's difficult not to respect someone who is chasing a dream.
- Listening to those around you. Taking the time to digest what others say is vital and can amplify your message.
- Staying true to your instincts. If you compromise your vision because of others' pressure, you lose control, and *chip, chip, chip*—suddenly the end result isn't what you envisioned.

Capra had a vision of what he wanted this movie to look and sound like, including its texture and tone, and he didn't deviate from it—even if he had to push through challenges. You have to do the same. Your vision, for whatever you're pursuing, must be consistent from top to bottom. You are the only one who sees the whole picture. Make sure it develops in the way you intended.

For example, if you're a business owner, everything about your business from start to finish must be focused and complementary, from your business plan to your marketing materials to your final product to the way you interact with your customers. Even your employees, perhaps the most critical piece of the puzzle, must fit into the big picture seamlessly. You may want a more formal suit-and-tie appearance for your employees rather than a casual presentation. You can set the tone and expectation for how your business presents itself!

People will likely come and go and add their input or opinion on whatever it is you're pursuing. Some of those interactions may be difficult, especially if you're having a hard time getting people to see your vision. But in the end, for whatever your dream might be, you must have the last word. As Capra understood, you can't have execs making one movie, writers making another, producers pushing yet a different direction, the cinematographer leaning into his own vision, the music score communicating something else, and you, *the director*, steering the ship—all this pushing and pulling at the same time. It must be one director, one film.

Or in your case—one person, one project, one vision.

At every milestone, stay true to your dream. Surround yourself with people who are on the same page as you. If, down the road, you find you're not getting what you want or that you've deviated off course, discuss your concerns with the other parties, and if things don't change, cut your losses and stay the course. It's better in the long run.

Despite his strong sense of vision, Capra kept an open mind for new opportunities. For instance, while scouting locations, he learned that there was a swimming pool under the gym floor at Beverly Hills High School. He immediately wrote it into the script, resulting in that unforgettable scene where George and Mary unknowingly dance right into the pool. That scene is iconic and wouldn't have happened without Capra's openness to opportunity.

Capra believed that *It's a Wonderful Life* was the best film he had ever made, but it was a box office disappointment, grossing only $3.3 million. Critical response was mixed.

Bosley Crowther of *The New York Times* wrote:

> The weakness of this picture ... is its illusory concept of life. Mr. Capra's nice people are charming, his small town is a quite beguiling place and his pattern for solving problems is most optimistic and facile. But somehow they all resemble theatrical attitudes rather than average realities.

New Yorker critic John McCarten was even harsher, calling the story "so mincing as to border on baby talk" and pitying Henry Travers for "God help him, [having] the job of portraying Mr. Stewart's guardian angel."

Capra didn't care whether critics praised or panned *It's a Wonderful Life*.

He might have agreed with Teddy Roosevelt's thoughts:

> It is not the critic who counts; not the man who points out how the strong man stumbles, or where the doer of deeds could have done them better. The credit belongs to the man who is actually in the arena, whose face is marred by dust and sweat and blood; who strives valiantly; who errs, who comes short again and again, because there is no effort without error or shortcoming; but who does actually strive to do the deeds;

who knows the great enthusiasms, the great devotions; who spends himself in a worthy cause; who at the best knows in the end the triumph of high achievement, and who at the worst, if he fails, at least fails while daring greatly, so that his place shall never be with those cold and timid souls who neither know victory nor defeat.

Approach your work that way. Put your imprint, your signature, on it. It's your money, your time and effort, your passion. Do it your way and don't worry about what anyone else thinks! You're the one who will rise or fall.

In June 1996, Sheldon Leonard, who played Nick the bartender, was recording his thoughts about acting in *It's a Wonderful Life*. The footage was to be shown at an upcoming Donna Reed Festival, where we were saluting the movie's fiftieth anniversary.

The movie had long been a hit at this point, and Sheldon and I were talking about why its popularity had continued to grow so many years after its initial release.

Sheldon's conclusion? The movie never changed; the people changed.

Back in 1946, people had just returned from winning a war. They didn't need the message of *It's a Wonderful Life* then. They were high on victory and determination. But people in the years since have needed hope and inspiration. Watching George Bailey realize how much impact his one life has made can make audiences recognize their own purpose and importance, to see that they, too, can make a difference no matter how big or small their life is.

Viewers today resonate with the strong themes of family and community in the film and its emphasis on the support and love George receives from his family and from the supportive community of Bedford Falls, highlighting the vital role of strong relationships, particularly in times of need. Lord knows we all experience that today.

It seems Capra was right after all. *It's a Wonderful Life* indeed has become one of the greatest films of all time.

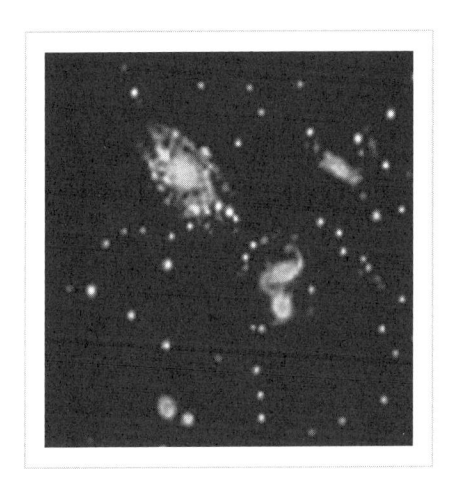

SCENE 2

An Answer to Our Prayers

The prayer of a righteous person is powerful and effective.

JAMES 5:16

FADE IN - NIGHT SEQUENCE

SERIES OF SHOTS of various streets and buildings in the town of Bedford Falls, somewhere in New York State. The streets are deserted, and snow is falling. It is Christmas Eve. Over the above scenes we hear voices praying:

> GOWER'S VOICE
> I owe everything to George Bailey. Help him, dear Father.

> MARTINI'S VOICE
> Joseph, Jesus and Mary. Help my friend Mr. Bailey.

> MRS. BAILEY'S VOICE
> Help my son George tonight.

> BERT'S VOICE
> He never thinks about himself, God; that's why he's in trouble.

> ERNIE'S VOICE
> George is a good guy. Give him a break, God.

AN ANSWER TO OUR PRAYERS

> **MARY'S VOICE**
> I love him, dear Lord. Watch over him tonight.
>
> **JANIE'S VOICE**
> Please, God. Something's the matter with Daddy.
>
> **ZUZU'S VOICE**
> Please bring Daddy back.

Notice how the people of Bedford Falls pray.

These people—whose lives have been touched in some way big or small by George Bailey and his kindness—seek God's help on behalf of a man they truly care about. George has spent his life looking after them—even at the expense of his own dreams. They prayerfully and humbly bring George before God and ask God for His help.

Although God surely already knows everything about George and what is going on in his mind and heart, the prayers of the people of Bedford Falls are powerful. For as the Bible says, "Where two or three gather in my name, there am I with them" (Matthew 18:20).

I believe in the power of prayer in just this way—that concerted prayer arouses power in heavenly places. I've experienced it myself many times. Maybe I had a great plan about something that would solve all my problems. And I wanted it to happen *now*.

But guess what? Most of the time, things haven't worked out that way. My prayers are rarely answered on my schedule. And it can be frustrating!

I talk to God all the time. I pray about the dreams I hope will come true. About the people I love. About everything, really. And God does answer. But oftentimes the answer is later—and sometimes it comes in a way I didn't expect.

And thank God for that! Because God's answers are always worth the wait and are often bigger and better than how I hoped He'd answer. He'll do the same for you. Talk to Him. Be open to His timing instead of yours. And the rewards will be more than you could dream of.

The prayers from the people of Bedford Falls are so beautiful and sincere.

"Give him a break, God."

"Something's the matter with Daddy."

"I love him, dear Lord."

"Help my son George tonight."

What a reminder to us that we can go to God with anything at all and in the simplest language, and He is always ready to listen and answer.

SCENE 3

The Hero Inside of You

If everybody was satisfied with himself, there would be no heroes.

—MARK TWAIN

EXT. FROZEN RIVER AND HILL - DAY - 1919

CLOSE SHOT

Group of boys. They are preparing to slide down the hill on large shovels. One of them makes the slide and shoots out onto the ice of a frozen river at the bottom of the hill. . . .

Series of shots as four or five boys make the slide down the hill and out onto the ice. As each boy comes down the others applaud.

CLOSE SHOT

George Bailey at bottom of slide.

>   GEORGE
>   (through megaphone)
>   And here comes the scare-baby, my kid
>   brother, Harry Bailey.

CLOSE SHOT - HARRY

On top of hill, preparing to make his slide.

                    HARRY
     I'm not scared.

                    BOYS
                  (ad lib)
     Come on, Harry! Attaboy, Harry!

MEDIUM SHOT

Harry makes his slide very fast. He passes
the marks made by the other boys, and his
shovel takes him onto the thin ice at the
bend of the river. The ice breaks, and
Harry disappears into the water.

CLOSE SHOT - GEORGE

                    GEORGE
     I'm coming, Harry.

MEDIUM SHOT

George jumps into the water and grabs Harry.
As he starts to pull him out he yells:

                    GEORGE
     Make a chain, gang! A chain!

WIDER ANGLE

The other boys lie flat on the ice,
forming a human chain. When George
reaches the edge with Harry in his arms,
they pull them both to safety.

THE HEART OF IT'S A WONDERFUL LIFE

George and his friends form a chain to save Harry.

JOSEPH'S VOICE
```
George saved his brother's life that
day. But he caught a bad cold which
infected his left ear. Cost him his
hearing in that ear. It was weeks
before he could return to his after-
school job at old man Gower's drugstore.
```

What does it take to be a hero? George experienced being a hero early in his life, as a child, when he saved his brother, Harry, from drowning in the icy pond. Because of that heroic action by young George, Harry goes on to save lives during World War II and even receives the Congressional Medal of Honor.

Later in the story, when a despairing George wishes he had never been born, it becomes clear that no George would've meant no Harry—because George wouldn't have been there to rescue him from the icy waters. And no Harry means those lives wouldn't have been saved on that transport. No Medal of Honor would have been awarded.

The consequences of that one heroic act by young George on that wintry day are huge and carry forward for years to come. I love this quote from the *Mishnah*, the first known written collection of Jewish oral traditions: "A person who saves one soul is considered as if he has saved the entire world."

George Bailey exemplifies that. So what makes a hero?

According to *Merriam-Webster*, a hero is "a person admired for achievements and noble qualities" or "one who shows great courage." Heroes can be powerful role models who help us develop personal values, build self-identity, and set goals. They're people who do what must be done, regardless of the consequences. They commit to character and integrity, to a mix of both bravery and humility.

We've all had childhood heroes, people who made meaningful contributions to our early lives and developed what our sense of heroism is. My childhood hero was Roy Rogers, "King of the Cowboys." Of course, I shared him with millions of other kids who sat in darkened theaters on Saturday afternoons, watching as he rode across the silver screen on his beautiful golden palomino, Trigger.

Roy was the model of fair play, someone who righted wrongs. By the end of his movies, he had made the world a better place. You knew you were safe if Roy was there.

Patrick Swayze, Roy Rogers, and me.

Many years later, as an adult, I met Roy Rogers and worked closely with him on a movie project. With Roy, what you saw was what you got. He didn't say one thing and do another. There were no skeletons in his closet. Roy was truly a hero, and it was so meaningful to see a man who matched the legend he had been in my mind since childhood.

I also worked for and with Gene Autry for six years. He turned out to be a longtime friend. I would sit in the box seats next to him at the ballpark when he owned his baseball team, the Angels. Quite a guy. He was always there for me. The original "Singing Cowboy," Gene recorded many hit songs, including "Rudolph the Red-Nosed Reindeer," "Back in the Saddle Again," "Here Comes Santa Claus," "You Are My Sunshine," "Be Honest with Me" (that last one was nominated for an Academy Award for Best Original Song), and many, many others.

I played Tagg Oakley in the popular *Annie Oakley* television series, which was produced by Autry's company, Flying A Productions. It aired on CBS sydication from 1954 to 1957. Autry, too, was a hero to millions of kids. And like Rogers, the man Gene was on the screen was who he was in person.

Touring with Gene Autry for ten weeks at rodeos and state fairs, 1958.

If you shook Gene's or Roy's hands on a deal, it was as good as any contract a high-powered lawyer might draw up. There must have been something in the water back then.

Imagine if your childhood hero had never been born. How different would you be? What did you learn from them that shaped who you are today?

If, like George, you had the opportunity to see life as if you had never existed, I think you'd quickly realize how important each of us is and what life-changing powers we possess. Each of us has the potential to be a hero to someone—and to alter their entire future.

The actor Christopher Reeve, best known as Superman in the big-budget *Superman* movies, suffered an equestrian accident that left him paralyzed from the neck down. In the 2024 documentary *Super/Man: The Christopher Reeve Story*, he shares in his own words his definition of a hero:

> "What is a hero? My answer was that a hero is someone who commits a courageous action without considering the consequences," Reeve is heard saying in the trailer. "Now my definition is completely different. I think a hero is an ordinary individual who finds the strength to persevere and endure in spite of overwhelming obstacles."

This superstar, a man gifted with great physical prowess, had his entire life changed in an instant—and his perception of heroism changed as well. As I've aged, I think my definition of *hero* has likely shifted as well. My hope is that at some point, we all have a moment like George did—where we realize that every person, regardless of status or wealth or fame, can be a hero and change not only their own life but the lives of others around them.

How has your definition of *hero* changed over the years?

SCENE 4

Follow Your Dreams

A hunch is creativity trying to tell you something.

—FRANK CAPRA

INT. DRUGSTORE - DAY

CLOSE SHOT - GEORGE AND MARY AT FOUNTAIN

> GEORGE
> Made up your mind yet?

> MARY
> I'll take chocolate.

George puts some chocolate ice cream in a dish.

> GEORGE
> With coconuts?

> MARY
> I don't like coconuts.

> GEORGE
> You don't like coconuts! Say, brainless, don't you know where coconuts come from? Lookit here - from Tahiti - Fiji Islands, the Coral Sea!

He pulls a magazine from his pocket and shows it to her.

                    MARY
          A new magazine! I never saw it before.

                    GEORGE
          Of course you never. Only us explorers
          can get it. I've been nominated for
          membership in the National Geographic
          Society.

He leans down to finish scooping out the
ice cream, his deaf ear toward her. She
leans over, speaking softly.

CLOSE SHOT

Mary, whispering.

                    MARY
          Is this the ear you can't hear on?
          George Bailey, I'll love you till the
          day I die.

She draws back quickly and looks down,
terrified at what she has said.

CLOSE SHOT - GEORGE AND MARY

                    GEORGE
          I'm going out exploring some day, you
          watch. And I'm going to have a couple
          of harems, and maybe three or four
          wives. Wait and see.

THE HEART OF IT'S A WONDERFUL LIFE

George had a dream early in life. He wanted to see the world. He wanted to build things. Even as a kid, this dream was planted firmly in his heart, and he was making plans to go after it.

I believe we're never given a dream without *also* being given the power to make that dream come true. Now, that statement might seem counterintuitive given that the way we see George's "dream" come true isn't linear. But when you hold on to that dream, when you live in integrity (like George's dad did, and like George ends up doing as well), when you work hard—in the end, it will all work out.

At the heart of George's dream to leave Bedford Falls is that he wants to *do something*, to *be someone*. Does that dream come true in the most literal sense? No. But George has something special—he is doing something and being someone right where he is. Only he doesn't know it yet.

George loses his opportunity to go to college after his father suddenly passes away. What does George do? He steps in and accomplishes a great deal for the townspeople by running the Building and Loan and living from his core of integrity.

George's next opportunity to make his big break slips through his fingers after Harry returns from college. But George carries on . . . and a dream he hadn't verbalized (or maybe even acknowledged) comes true as he and Mary fall in love and begin to build a life together.

As George reaches the pinnacle of his frustration and discontent in the movie, to the outside eye—and from George's disillusioned perspective—it appears that his dreams will never come true. He never left town to see the world. He never made it to college. He never really got a chance to build things. He didn't make his mark on the world.

What about you? Did you miss out on that promotion? But did something else come along that ended up being better?

Did that thing you believed you must absolutely have end up falling by the wayside?

Did that relationship fall apart? How does it look now in hindsight?

As it turns out, George in fact *did* have it all. It just didn't look like what he'd envisioned. He had a loving wife and children, a community that was grateful for him, and a mission to help others through the work of the Building and Loan. George's life was one that so many of us might long for!

If only we all could have a chance, like George, to witness how much our one small life has affected those around us. If only we would take a moment to see that we may be living our dream life after all, surrounded by family, friends, and love.

SCENE 5

Trust Your Instinct

❦

You have first an instinct, then an opinion, then a knowledge, as the plant has root, bud, and fruit. Trust the instinct to the end.

—RALPH WALDO EMERSON

INT. BACK ROOM DRUGSTORE - DAY

CLOSE SHOT - GEORGE AND GOWER

                GOWER
You lazy loafer!

                GEORGE
               (sobbing)
Mr. Gower, you don't know what you're doing. You put something wrong in those capsules. I know you're unhappy. You got that telegram, and you're upset. You put something bad in those capsules. It wasn't your fault, Mr. Gower . . .

George pulls the little box out of his pocket. Gower savagely rips it away from him, breathing heavily, staring at the boy venomously.

           GEORGE (CONT'D)
Just look and see what you did. Look at the bottle you took the powder from. It's poison! I tell you, it's poison! I know you feel bad . . . and . . .

George falters off, cupping his aching ear with a hand. Gower looks at the large brown bottle which has not been replaced on the shelf. He tears open the package, shakes the powder out of one of the capsules, cautiously tastes it, then abruptly throws the whole mess to the table and turns to look at George again. The boy is whimpering, hurt, frightened. Gower steps toward him.

               GEORGE (CONT'D)
     Don't hurt my sore ear again.

But this time Gower sweeps the boy to him in a hug and, sobbing hoarsely, crushes the boy in his embrace. George is crying too.

               GOWER
     No . . . No . . . No . . .

               GEORGE
     Don't hurt my ear again!

               GOWER
               (sobbing)
     Oh, George, George . . .

               GEORGE
     Mr. Gower, I won't ever tell anyone. I
     know what you're feeling. I won't ever
     tell a soul. Hope to die, I won't.

               GOWER
     Oh, George.

In 1984, I produced a movie for Disney called *Love Leads the Way*. It told the true story of the first Seeing Eye dog in America. These amazing dogs are trained to keep their humans safe. This means making sure their people don't walk into traffic, fall down a set of stairs, or succumb to other dangers that blind people might encounter.

In one of their classes, the dogs are taught something that might seem odd given that they're trained to follow commands to the letter. In this class the dogs are told to ignore a command—one that would jeopardize the safety of the human or the dog. The

The cast of Love Leads the Way *(left to right): Ernest Borgnine, Glynnis O'Connor, producer me, Ralph Bellamy, director Delbert Mann, Timothy Bottoms, Eva Marie Saint, and Pilot as Buddy, the First Lady of the Seeing Eye.*

dogs are taught how to react when unexpected trouble comes and the dog must disobey the owner in order to keep the owner safe. It's called *intelligent disobedience*. And through this very special learned skill, the Seeing Eye dog is able to protect its owner from a possible life-threating situation. It's truly remarkable.

George exhibits a bit of intelligent disobedience of his own when he disobeys Mr. Gower in delivering the poisoned prescription. If George hadn't disobeyed, the Blaine kid might have died. Mr. Gower likely would have gone to jail (on top of being devastated at the horrible mistake he had made). George took a big chance second-guessing his boss.

Young George tried to ask his dad for advice. But that didn't work out because Mr. Potter was there. So what did George do? He used common sense. Even though he was young, George was forced to think on his feet and disobey authority for the greater good. Mr. Gower's abilities were clouded by his grief. Thank goodness young George listened to his gut and made that decision!

George not only saves a child's life but also saves Mr. Gower's reputation and his future. And in the middle of a tense and hurtful moment with Mr. Gower, George shows a great deal of compassion for the grieving man. Despite Mr. Gower's behavior, George forgives him. He promises he'll never tell, and he doesn't.

This glimpse into George's character and integrity, even at such a young age, reveals so much about the kind of man George will become. And it sets the stage for how George will be prepared to confront challenges in his life going forward.

SCENE 6

No Regrets

Make sure you tell the people you love that you love them. Loudly and often. You never know when it might be too late.

—UNKNOWN

INT. BAILEY DINING ROOM - NIGHT

CLOSE SHOT

George and his father, eating at the table. There is a great similarity and a great understanding between them.

> POP
> Hope you have a good trip, George. Uncle Billy and I are going to miss you.

> GEORGE
> I'm going to miss you, too, Pop. What's the matter? You look tired.

> POP
> Oh, I had another tussle with Potter today.

> GEORGE
> Oh . . .

> POP
> I thought when we put him on the Board of Directors, he'd ease up on us a little bit.

GEORGE
I wonder what's eating that old money-grubbing buzzard anyway?

POP
Oh, he's a sick man. Frustrated and sick. Sick in his mind, sick in his soul, if he has one. Hates everybody that has anything that he can't have. Hates us mostly, I guess. . . .

POP
You know, George, wish we could send Harry to college with you. Your mother and I talked it over half the night.

GEORGE
We have that all figured out. You see, Harry'll take my job at the Building and Loan, work there four years, then he'll go.

POP
He's pretty young for that job.

GEORGE
Well, no younger than I was.

POP
Maybe you were born older, George.

GEORGE
How's that?

POP
I say, maybe you were born older. I suppose you've decided what you're going to do when you get out of college.

GEORGE
Oh, well, you know what I've always talked about - build things . . . design new buildings - plan modern cities - all that stuff I was talking about.

POP
Still after that first million before you're thirty.

GEORGE
No, I'll settle for half that in cash . . .

POP
Of course, it's just a hope, but you wouldn't consider coming back to the Building and Loan, would you? . . .

GEORGE
Oh, now, Pop, I couldn't. I couldn't face being cooped up for the rest of my life in a shabby little office.

He stops, realizing that he has hurt his father.

GEORGE (CONT'D)
Oh, I'm sorry, Pop. I didn't mean that remark, but this business of nickels and dimes and spending all your life trying to figure out how to save three cents on a length of pipe . . . I'd go crazy. I want to do something big and something important.

POP
(quietly)
You know, George, I feel that in a small way we are doing something important. Satisfying a fundamental urge. It's deep in the race for a man to want his own roof and walls and fireplace, and we're helping him get those things in our shabby little office.

GEORGE
(unhappily)
I know, Dad. I wish I felt . . . But I've been hoarding pennies like a miser in order to . . . Most of my friends have already finished college. I just feel like if I don't get away, I'd bust.

POP
Yes . . . Yes . . . You're right, son.

GEORGE
You see what I mean, don't you, Pop?

> POP
> This town is no place for any man unless he's willing to crawl to Potter. You've got talent, son. You get yourself an education. Then get out of here.
>
> GEORGE
> Pop, do you want a shock? I think you're a great guy.
>
> To cover his embarrassment, he looks toward the kitchen door and calls:
>
> GEORGE (CONT'D)
> Oh, did you hear that, Annie?
>
> CLOSE SHOT
>
> Annie listening through glass in door.
>
> ANNIE
> I heard it. About time one of you lunkheads said it.

Expressing our emotions can be so difficult! Especially for men.

Despite George's aspirations to leave Bedford Falls and see the world, his pop is his hero. Owner of Bailey Brothers Building and Loan, Pa Bailey had lived an honorable life. George had great respect for his dad, who is a decent man with great integrity.

George could only hope that people might look up to him one day the way they do his pop.

This conversation is the last time George speaks to his father. Just a few hours later, George will learn that his dad has had a stroke and died. In these final moments together, filled with honest conversation, George has the chance to tell his father that he thinks Pa Bailey is "a great guy." And it is a moment when we see George realize that his dad has made such a big impact despite never leaving Bedford Falls.

Annie, the maid, humorously points out this special moment between father and son. And what a conversation to have when, only hours later, George's dad is gone. George will never forget that talk.

I was lucky to have a similar talk with my dad before it was too late.

My dad had been in the hospital for a couple days for some tests. I would visit in the evening to bring him dessert and to wish him good night. That night, I leaned down to give him a hug. As I stood back up, he said, "We never did that much, did we?"

"No, we didn't," I said.

That was the only time my dad and I approached a conversation in that vein. We had gotten along just fine. He even prop mastered for two movies I produced. But we weren't demonstrative in our affection for each other. I'm so grateful we had that brief moment of connection. It was a shock to me when my dad brought it up, but I'm so glad those words were said.

Jimmy Stewart often said that his dad, who served in both the Spanish-American War and World War I, was a major influence in his life and had the biggest impact on him. In other words, his dad was his hero.

We never know when a conversation might be our last. When an opportunity to tell someone we love them, that we're proud of them, that we're grateful for them, might be the final moment to say those words that matter most. When leaning in for a hug will be the catalyst to a conversation before it's too late.

Watch for those moments. Listen to that voice that tells you to come close, to say the words to the people who matter most.

SCENE 7

Dance by the Light of the Moon

Above all, every man is born with an inner capacity to take him as far as his imagination can dream or envision—providing he is free to dream and envision.

—FRANK CAPRA

EXT. TREE - LINED RESIDENTIAL STREET - NIGHT

MEDIUM CLOSE SHOT - GEORGE AND MARY

The night is warm with a bright moon. George is dressed in jersey sweater and oversize football pants that keep wanting to come down. Mary is in an old white bath robe. Each is carrying their wet clothes tied into a bundle that leaves a trail of dripping water. As they near the camera we hear them singing:

> GEORGE AND MARY
> (singing)
> Buffalo Gals can't you come out tonight. Can't you come out tonight. Can't you come out tonight. Buffalo Gals can't you come out tonight and dance by the light of the moon.

> GEORGE
> Hot dog! Just like an organ.

> MARY
> Beautiful.

CAMERA MOVES WITH them as they
proceed down the street. . . .

Holding her hand, George moves in closer
to Mary.

          GEORGE (CONT'D)
  Hey - hey, Mary.

Mary turns away from him, singing
"Buffalo Gals":

          MARY
         (singing)
  As I was lumbering down the
  street . . .

George looks after her; then picks up a
rock from the street.

          GEORGE
  Okay, then, I'll throw a rock at the
  old Granville house.

          MARY
  Oh, no, don't. I love that old house.

MEDIUM LONG SHOT - OLD HOUSE

It is a weather-beaten, old-fashioned
two-storied house that once was no doubt
resplendent.

                    GEORGE
No. You see, you make a wish and then
try and break some glass. You got to
be a pretty good shot nowadays, too.

MEDIUM CLOSEUP - GEORGE AND MARY

George and Mary at the Granville house at 320 Sycamore Street.

                    MARY
Oh, no, George, don't. It's full of
romance, that old place. I'd like to
live in it.

                    GEORGE
In that place?

MARY
Uh-huh.

GEORGE
I wouldn't live in it as a ghost. Now watch . . . right on the second floor there.

MEDIUM LONG SHOT - OLD HOUSE

George hurls the rock at the house. We hear the SOUND of a window breaking. . . .

CLOSEUP - GEORGE AND MARY

MARY
What'd you wish, George?

GEORGE
Well, not just one wish. A whole hatful, Mary. I know what I'm going to do tomorrow and the next day and the next year and the year after that. I'm shaking the dust of this crummy little town off my feet and I'm going to see the world. Italy, Greece, the Parthenon, the Colosseum. Then I'm coming back here and go to college and see what they know . . . and then I'm going to build things. I'm gonna build air fields. I'm gonna build skyscrapers a hundred stories high. I'm gonna build bridges a mile long . . .

George is coming to the conclusion that he has deeper feelings for Mary. He's sharing his hopes and dreams with her. He might be secretly in love but isn't comfortable telling her directly. Even the neighbor on the porch sees it when he yells to George, "Why don't you kiss her instead of talking her to death?"

George thinks, *Maybe I will.* He's starting to understand Mary has a genuine affection for him.

But all Mary has heard is George's dream about leaving Bedford Falls. Mary's own dreams look a little different. She'd love to live in that house someday. Something about it speaks to Mary's heart.

We get to see something special in this scene—a first glimpse of two people who may have a dream together that they're not aware of yet. A future that will bring them back to each other, back to this dilapidated house, and to a family with children. This memorable, romantic scene sets up George and Mary's future—even if they don't know it.

Have you experienced anything like this? A dream that doesn't come true? Or—and this can be so surprising—the realization with hindsight that life had a better dream for you that you weren't even aware of?

As we see later in the movie, if George's life had unfolded in the ways he intended, he would have missed out on so much beauty and love. And we get a small taste of it in this scene, as two young people dance by the light of the moon and share their hearts with each other.

SCENE 8

Stuck in Bedford Falls

All you can take with you is that which you've given away.

—PETER BAILEY

INT. BAILEY BUILDING AND LOAN OFFICE - DAY

CLOSE SHOT - DIRECTORS MEETING

There are about twelve directors seated around a long table. They are the substantial citizens of Bedford Falls: Dr. Campbell, a lawyer, an insurance agent, a real estate salesman, etc. Prominently seated among them is Henry F. Potter, his goon beside his wheelchair. Uncle Billy and George are seated among the directors. The Chairman of the Board is Dr. Campbell. They have folders and papers before them, on which they have been reporting. Before each of the directors there are individual reports for them to study. . . .

>DR. CAMPBELL
> Now we come to the real purpose of this meeting - to appoint a successor to our dear friend, Peter Bailey.

>POTTER
> Mr. Chairman, I'd like to get to my real purpose.

                    MAN
Wait just a minute now.

                  POTTER
Wait for what? I claim this institution
is not necessary to this town. Therefore,
Mr. Chairman, I make a motion to dissolve
this institution and turn its assets and
liabilities over to the receiver.

                UNCLE BILLY
                  (angrily)
George, you hear what that buzzard . . .

                  LAWYER
Mr. Chairman, it's too soon after Peter
Bailey's death to discuss chloroforming
the Building and Loan.

                    MAN
Peter Bailey died three months ago. I
second Mr. Potter's motion.

                DR. CAMPBELL
Very well. In that case I'll ask the two
executive officers to withdraw.

Dr. Campbell rises from his seat. George and
Uncle Billy start to collect their papers
and leave the table.

            DR. CAMPBELL (CONT'D)
But before you go, I'm sure the
whole board wishes to express its

deep sorrow at the passing of Peter
Bailey.

GEORGE
Thank you very much.

DR. CAMPBELL
It was his faith and devotion that are
responsible for this organization.

POTTER
I'll go further than that. I'll say
that to the public Peter Bailey was
the Building and Loan.

Everyone looks at him surprised.

UNCLE BILLY
(trying to control himself)
Oh, that's fine, Potter, coming from
you, considering that you probably
drove him to his grave.

POTTER
Peter Bailey was not a business man.
That's what killed him. Oh, I don't
mean any disrespect to him, God rest
his soul. He was a man of high ideals,
so-called, but ideals without common
sense can ruin this town.
(picking up papers from table)
Now, you take this loan here to Ernie
Bishop . . . You know, that fellow that
sits around all day on his brains in

his taxi. You know . . . I happen to
know the bank turned down this loan, but
he comes here and we're building him a
house worth five thousand dollars. Why?

George is at the door of the office, holding
his coat and papers, ready to leave.

                    GEORGE
Well, I handled that, Mr. Potter. You
have all the papers there. His salary,
insurance. I can personally vouch for
his character.

                    POTTER
              (sarcastically)
A friend of yours?

                    GEORGE
Yes, sir.

                    POTTER
You see, if you shoot pool with some
employee here, you can come and
borrow money. What does that get us? A
discontented, lazy rabble instead of a
thrifty working class. And all because a
few starry-eyed dreamers like Peter Bailey
stir them up and fill their heads with a
lot of impossible ideas. Now, I say . . .

George puts down his coat and comes around
to the table, incensed by what Potter is
saying about his father.

GEORGE

Just a minute - just a minute. Now, hold on, Mr. Potter. You're right when you say my father was no business man. I know that. Why he ever started this cheap, penny-ante Building and Loan, I'll never know. But neither you nor anybody else can say anything against his character, because his whole life was . . . Why, in the twenty-five years since he and Uncle Billy started this thing, he never once thought of himself. Isn't that right, Uncle Billy? He didn't save enough money to send Harry to school, let alone me. But he did help a few people get out of your slums, Mr. Potter. And what's wrong with that? Why . . . Here, you're all businessmen here. Doesn't it make them better citizens? Doesn't it make them better customers? You . . . you said . . . What'd you say just a minute ago? . . . They had to wait and save their money before they even ought to think of a decent home. Wait! Wait for what? Until their children grow up and leave them? Until they're so old and broken-down that they . . . Do you know how long it takes a working man to save five thousand dollars? Just remember this, Mr. Potter, that this rabble you're talking about . . . they do most of the working and paying and living and dying in this community.

Well, is it too much to have them
work and pay and live and die in a
couple of decent rooms and a bath?
Anyway, my father didn't think so.
People were human beings to him, but
to you, a warped, frustrated old man,
they're cattle. Well, in my book he
died a much richer man than you'll
ever be!

POTTER

I'm not interested in your book. I'm
talking about the Building and Loan.

GEORGE

I know very well what you're talking
about. You're talking about something
you can't get your fingers on, and
it's galling you. That's what you're
talking about, I know.
    (to the Board)
Well, I've said too much. I . . .
You're the Board here. You do what you
want with this thing. Just one thing
more, though. This town needs this
measly one-horse institution if only
to have someplace where people can
come without crawling to Potter. Come
on, Uncle Billy!

George leaves the room, followed by the
jubilant Uncle Billy. Potter's face is
grim with hatred. The "frustrated old
man" remark was gall in his veins.

                        POTTER
    Sentimental hogwash! I want my motion . . .

INT. OUTER OFFICE - BUILDING AND LOAN - DAY

MEDIUM CLOSE SHOT - GEORGE AND THE OTHERS

                        GEORGE
              (indicating Board room)
    I wonder what's going on in there?

                      UNCLE BILLY
    Oh, never mind. Don't worry about that.
    They're putting us out of business. So
    what? I can get another job. I'm only
    fifty-five.

                      COUSIN TILLY
    Fifty-six!

                      UNCLE BILLY
    Go on - go on. Hey, look, you gave up
    your boat trip, now you don't want to
    miss college too, do you?

Dr. Campbell comes running out, all excited.

                      DR. CAMPBELL
    George! George! They voted Potter down!
    They want to keep it going!

Cousin Eustace, Cousin Tilly and Uncle Billy
cheer wildly. Dr. Campbell and George shake
hands.

UNCLE BILLY
Whoopee!

DR. CAMPBELL
But they've got one condition - only one condition.

GEORGE
What's that?

DR. CAMPBELL
That's the best part of it. They've appointed George here as executive secretary to take his father's place.

GEORGE
Oh, no! But, Uncle Billy . . .

DR. CAMPBELL
You can keep him on. That's all right. As secretary you can hire anyone you like.

GEORGE
(emphatically)
Dr. Campbell, now let's get this thing straight. I'm leaving. I'm leaving right now. I'm going to school. This is my last chance. Uncle Billy here, he's your man.

DR. CAMPBELL
But, George, they'll vote with Potter otherwise.

THE HEART OF IT'S A WONDERFUL LIFE

He'll never get out of Bedford Falls.

Everything changed in the blink of an eye.

George had his suitcase packed and was ready to leave Bedford Falls. Ernie was waiting to take him to the train station. But instead of being on his way, George and his uncle Billy are now standing in front of the board of directors, pleading to keep the Building and Loan open.

The starry-eyed George who was sharing his big dreams with Mary just weeks before surely never imagined he'd be standing in front of a group of men, defending his father's good work in the community against Mr. Potter's efforts to shut down the Building and Loan.

But life has a way of surprising us. We make plans . . . and then fate walks in.

STUCK IN BEDFORD FALLS

George must have seen everything dissolving in front of his eyes. What about his trip? What about college? Staying in Bedford Falls—running the Building and Loan—wasn't his plan.

But he agrees to it. As the years pass, more of his dreams seem to slip away. George gives his saved money to Harry for college, with the understanding that Harry will return and take over the Building and Loan so George can leave town. But when Harry returns, he is married and has gotten a job offer from his father-in-law that will take him away from Bedford Falls.

It all sinks in when George is standing there at the train depot and learns of Harry's opportunity. He hears the beckoning call of the train whistle, telling him he won't ever be leaving Bedford Falls—not to go to college, not to see the world, not to build things.

George will be staying in Bedford Falls. He's stuck at the Building and Loan.

But something in George keeps a glimmer of his dream alive. He doesn't stop thinking of designing and building. He works hard on his plans for Bailey Park, to provide housing for low-income people. And that persistence likely fuels George during a time when it feels like his dreams were coming to an end.

Calvin Coolidge is often credited with this quote: "Nothing in this world can take the place of persistence. . . . The slogan 'press on' has solved and always will solve the problems of the human race."

And despite George's unplanned-for future, he persists. He does meaningful work in his small town. He helps people.

And although he doesn't realize it, he, too, is becoming a hero for many people who love him.

SCENE 9

Lasso the Moon

❧

What is it you want, Mary? You want the moon? If you do, just say the word, I'll throw a lasso around it and pull it down for you.

—GEORGE BAILEY

INT. HATCH HOME - NIGHT

MEDIUM CLOSE SHOT

          MARY
         (calling)
Geo . . . George, Sam wants to speak to you.

She hands the instrument to George.

          GEORGE
Hello, Sam.

INT. SAM'S NEW YORK OFFICE - NIGHT

MEDIUM CLOSE SHOT

Sam is seated at his desk, while a couple of his friends are nearby, with highballs in their hands.

          SAM
        (into phone)
Well, George Baileyoffski! Hey, a fine pal you are. What're you trying to do? Steal my girl?

INT. HATCH HALL - NIGHT

MEDIUM CLOSE SHOT - GEORGE AND MARY

               GEORGE
            (into phone)
What do you mean? Nobody's trying to steal your girl. Here . . . here's Mary.

              SAM'S VOICE
No, wait a minute. Wait a minute. I want to talk to both of you. Tell Mary to get on the extension.

               GEORGE
            (to Mary)
Here. You take it. You tell him. . . .

George and Mary huddle around the phone, talking to Sam Wainwright.

                    MARY
          We can both hear. Come here.

Mary takes the telephone from George and
holds it so that of necessity George's
cheek is almost against hers. He is very
conscious of her proximity.

                    MARY
                  (on phone)
          We're listening, Sam.

                  SAM'S VOICE
          I have a big deal coming up that's
          going to make us all rich. George, you
          remember that night in Martini's bar
          when you told me you read someplace
          about making plastics out of soybeans?

                    GEORGE
          Huh? Yeah - yeah - yeah . . .
          soybeans. Yeah.

                  SAM'S VOICE
          Well, Dad's snapped up the idea. He's
          going to build a factory outside of
          Rochester. How do you like that?

Mary is watching George interestedly.
George is very conscious of her, close to
him.

                    GEORGE
          Rochester? Well, why Rochester?

SAM'S VOICE
Well, why not? Can you think of anything better?

GEORGE
Oh, I don't know . . . why not right here? You remember that old tool and machinery works? You tell your father he can get that for a song. And all the labor he wants, too. Half the town was thrown out of work when they closed down.

SAM'S VOICE
That so? Well, I'll tell him. Hey, that sounds great! Oh, baby, I knew you'd come through. Now, here's the point. Mary, Mary, you're in on this too. Now listen. Have you got any money?

GEORGE
Money? Yeah . . . well, a little.

SAM'S VOICE
Well, now listen. I want you to put every cent you've got into our stock, you hear? And George, I may have a job for you; that is, unless you're still married to that broken-down Building and Loan. This is the biggest thing since radio, and I'm letting you in on the ground floor. Oh, Mary . . . Mary . . .

                    MARY

    (nervously)
    I'm here.

                SAM'S VOICE
    Would you tell that guy I'm giving him
    the chance of a lifetime, you hear? The
    chance of a lifetime.

As Mary listens, she turns to look at
George, her lips almost on his lips.

                    MARY
    (whispering)
    He says it's the chance of a lifetime.

George can stand it no longer. He drops
the phone with a crash, grabs Mary by the
shoulders and shakes her. Mary begins to
cry.

                   GEORGE
    (fiercely)
    Now you listen to me! I don't want
    any plastics! I don't want any ground
    floors, and I don't want to get married
    - ever - to anyone! You understand
    that? I want to do what I want to do.
    And you you're . . . .and you're . . . .

He pulls her to him in a fierce embrace.

George has learned a lot in his years running the Building and Loan. He knows business, so when his good friend Sam asks for George's advice on a business opportunity, George immediately sees the big picture.

But this scene isn't about George's business sense or some big financial windfall. This scene is about George and Mary's love.

Let me give some insider information on what Capra was setting up with this phone scene.

The scene starts with George showing up at Mary's house. There is already tension between them, but neither can find the words to say how they feel. The ringing of the phone as George is leaving is annoying, adding to that tension. And when the two of them each place an ear at the receiver, their faces nearly touching, that tension only builds.

Capra set it up perfectly. If these two people are ever going to get together, it'll be now. There are unspoken words. George and Mary are side by side, perhaps physically closer than they've ever been. And Sam is on the other end of the line with an opportunity that could change George's life—could get him out of this little town and one step closer to his dreams.

Jimmy Stewart didn't want to film that scene. He had been putting it off for a while. He hadn't shared a kiss on-screen in a long time. Finally, Capra said enough is enough.

"Jimmy, it's just two lips coming together. Let's do it."

For the time, this scene was considered quite racy. The Hays Code, officially known as the Motion Picture Production Code,

*Jimmy Stewart and Donna Reed prepare for the
big kiss. Frank Capra is in the foreground.*

was a set of movie-industry guidelines from 1930 to 1968 with a goal to restrict content that it deemed inappropriate. This kiss was considered steamy enough to be in violation.

When Capra yelled "cut!" after the filming, the script girl said they had left out a page of dialogue.

"With technique like that, who needs dialogue?" Capra said.

From this point forward, the trajectory of George's life seems to have permanently landed him in Bedford Falls. But it's a future with Mary...

SCENE 10

A Run on the Bank

If you fail to plan, you are planning to fail.

—UNKNOWN

George faces anxious customers.

INT. OUTER OFFICE - BUILDING AND LOAN - DAY

MEDIUM CLOSE SHOT

More people have crowded around the counter. Their muttering stops and they stand silent and grim. There is panic in their faces. . . .

                    GEORGE
  Tom! Tom! Randall! Now wait . . . now
  listen . . . now listen to me. I beg

A RUN ON THE BANK

of you not to do this thing. If Potter gets hold of this Building and Loan there'll never be another decent house built in this town. He's already got charge of the bank. He's got the bus line. He's got the department stores. And now he's after us. Why? Well, it's very simple. Because we're cutting in on his business, that's why. And because he wants to keep you living in his slums and paying the kind of rent he decides.

The people are still trying to get out, but some of them have stood still, listening to him. George has begun to make an impression on them.

GEORGE (CONT'D)
Joe, you lived in one of his houses, didn't you? Well, have you forgotten? Have you forgotten what he charged you for that broken-down shack?
(to Ed)
Here, Ed. You know, you remember last year when things weren't going so well, and you couldn't make your payments. You didn't lose your house, did you? Do you think Potter would have let you keep it?
(turns to address the room again)
Can't you understand what's happening here? Don't you see what's happening? Potter isn't selling. Potter's buying!

And why? Because we're panicky and he's not. That's why. He's picking up some bargains. Now, we can get through this thing all right. We've got to stick together, though. We've got to have faith in each other.

                    MRS. THOMPSON
But my husband hasn't worked in over a year, and I need money.

                    WOMAN
How am I going to live until the bank opens?

                    MAN
I got doctor bills to pay.

                    MAN
I need cash.

                    MAN
Can't feed my kids on faith.

During this scene Mary has come up behind the counter. Suddenly, as the people once more start moving toward the door, she holds up a roll of bills and calls out

                    MARY
How much do you need?

George jumps over the counter and takes the money from Mary.

Mary offers her and George's honeymoon funds to stop the bank run and save the Building and Loan.

GEORGE

Hey! I got two thousand dollars! Here's two thousand dollars. This'll tide us over until the bank reopens.
    (to Tom)
All right, Tom, how much do you need?

TOM
    (doggedly)
Two hundred and forty-two dollars!

GEORGE
    (pleading)
Aw, Tom, just enough to tide you over till the bank reopens.

TOM

I'll take two hundred and forty-two dollars.

George starts rapidly to count out the money. Tom throws his passbook on the counter.

> GEORGE
> There you are.

> TOM
> That'll close my account.

> GEORGE
> Your account's still here. That's a loan.

Mary turns and slips out through the crowd, followed by Ernie. George hands the two hundred and forty-two dollars to Tom, and speaks to Ed, the next in line.

> GEORGE (CONT'D)
> Okay. All right, Ed?

> ED
> I got three hundred dollars here, George.

Uncle Billy takes out his wallet and takes out all the cash he's got.

> GEORGE
> Aw, now, Ed . . . what'll it take till the bank reopens? What do you need?

> ED
> Well, I suppose twenty dollars.

A RUN ON THE BANK

                   GEORGE
Twenty dollars. Now you're talking.
Fine. Thanks, Ed.
   (to Mrs. Thompson, next in line)
All right, now, Mrs. Thompson. How much
do you want?

                MRS. THOMPSON
But it's your own money, George.

                   GEORGE
Never mind about that. How much do you
want?

                MRS. THOMPSON
I can get along with twenty, all right.

                   GEORGE
        (counting it out)
Twenty dollars.

                MRS. THOMPSON
And I'll sign a paper.

                   GEORGE
You don't have to sign anything. I know
you'll pay it back when you can. That's
okay.
       (to woman next in line)
All right, Mrs. Davis.

                 MRS. DAVIS
Could I have seventeen-fifty?

THE HEART OF IT'S A WONDERFUL LIFE

>   GEORGE
>   Seven . . .
>   (he kisses her)
>   Bless your heart. Of course you can
>   have it. You got fifty cents?
>   (counting)
>   Seven . . .

The town bank, run by Mr. Potter, has suddenly called the loan on Bailey Brothers Building and Loan. It's George and Mary's wedding day, and Uncle Billy has just shared this news with a shocked George.

George calms his nervous depositors, who are fearful that they won't be able to withdraw the funds they have deposited there, by assuring them that if they keep their faith in the institution, times will improve. He feels a great sense of responsibility for the residents of Bedford Falls. George has been in the business of nickel and dimes and has spent most of his life trying to save three cents on a length of pipe.

Today, *It's a Wonderful Life* is often interpreted as a powerful reminder about the importance of community, the small, meaningful actions that can change lives, and the impact one person can have on others even while facing personal challenges. It highlights the often-overlooked significance of contributing to the well-being of your community rather than chasing individual wealth and success. And it's a reminder we need!

We've been talking about Bailey Brothers Building and Loan

for the entire book, but what the heck is a Building and Loan anyway?

During the 1920s, at the beginning of the movie, Building and Loans were huge. But by the end of the movie, right after World War II, most had already gone out of business or had been converted into Savings and Loans. Building and Loans were major mortgage lenders before the war, holding half of all residential mortgages. Their numbers grew rapidly, but they remained small cooperatives, like Bailey Brothers. Investors provided funding but often wanted quick withdrawals, leading to financial instability. Freezing withdrawals ultimately led to the institutions' downfall. By 1950, most had vanished or become S&Ls, which thrived until a crisis in the late 1980s. Despite their flaws, Building and Loans slowed foreclosures during the Great Depression.

George knew it was critical for the community members to keep their money in the B&L. If Potter won this battle, there would never be a place where the common man could catch a break. Potter would own everything in Bedford Falls and could set his own prices. So George stuck to his convictions. He could have walked away from the mess that day and said, "Oh, to hell with this. It's keeping me from seeing the world. I have a chance to go. No one could blame me."

But he didn't. Mary suggested that they use their honeymoon money to help the depositors. They fought for the little guy. In doing so, George stalled his personal dream again—but he saved the futures of so many people in the community.

THE HEART OF IT'S A WONDERFUL LIFE

At the end of the day, Bailey Brothers Building and Loan is left with just two dollars to put back in the safe—Papa Dollar and Mama Dollar—with the hopes that they'll be able to make a way forward.

It's a new beginning, because they didn't let Potter win.

Celebrating Papa Dollar and Mama Dollar.

SCENE 11

Welcome to Bailey Park

Someone should keep reminding Mr. Average Man that he was born free, divine, strong; uncrushable by fate, society, or hell itself; and that he is a child of God, equal heir to all the bounties of God; and that goodness is riches, kindness is power, and freedom is glory.

—FRANK CAPRA

EXT. BAILEY PARK - DAY

CLOSE SHOT

Sign hanging from a tree "Welcome to Bailey Park."

CAMERA PANS TO follow George's car and the old truck laden with furniture as they pass - we hear Martini's voice singing "O Sole Mio." Bailey Park is a district of new small houses, not all alike, but each individual. New lawns here and there, and young trees. It has the promise when built up of being a pleasant little middle class section.

                            WIPE TO:

EXT. MARTINI'S NEW HOUSE - DAY

MEDIUM CLOSE SHOT

George and Mary are on the porch of the new house, with the Martinis lined up before them.

WELCOME TO BAILEY PARK

Mary and George offer bread, wine, and salt to the Martinis at their new home.

>   GEORGE
> Mr. and Mrs. Martini, welcome home.

The Martinis cross themselves. . . .

>   MARY
> (to Mrs. Martini, giving her loaf of bread)
> Bread! That this house may never know
> hunger.

Mrs. Martini crosses herself.

>   MARY
>   (giving her salt)
> Salt! That life may always have flavor.

>   GEORGE
>   (handing bottle to Martini)
> And wine! That joy and prosperity may
> reign forever. Enter the Martini castle!

THE HEART OF IT'S A WONDERFUL LIFE

```
The Martinis cross themselves, shaking hands
all around. The kids enter, with screams of
delight. Mrs. Martini kisses Mary.
```

In this scene, Capra had an opportunity to salute his kind of people—average, hardworking, down-to-earth folk. George had worked to create opportunities in the community for people who might otherwise not have them. With Bailey Park, these folks had the chance to own a home and build a life for themselves. No person, regardless of circumstance, need be a failure. And everyone deserved a chance at a better life.

One of my favorite traditions at the It's A Wonderful Life Museum's festival in Seneca Falls each year is when we Bailey kids re-create the "bread, salt, wine" scene from the movie,

Me, little Violet (Jeanine Ann Roose), Janie Bailey (Carol Coombs Mueller), Zuzu Bailey (Karolyn Grimes), and Seneca Falls' newest Habitat House owners, the Riveras. Menzo Case is at the far right.

WELCOME TO BAILEY PARK

welcoming a family to their new Habitat for Humanity home. There is something so special about both reliving this scene and being a witness to a new start for a family.

This tradition was established by one of our all-time most generous Seneca Falls donors, Menzo Case.

I asked Fred Capozzi, board member of the museum and former police chief, to put something together to honor Mr. Case, with whom he was close. Here's what he shared:

> Habitat for Humanity in Seneca County was instrumentally developed by a neighborhood banker and president of Generation Bank of Seneca Falls, Mr. Menzo Case.
>
> Menzo passed away in October of 2023, but his passion for helping those in need lives on with the many Habitat for Humanity homes he helped build.
>
> Menzo believed new homeowners should be invested by helping work on, or putting sweat equity into, the building of their new home. Menzo was a huge supporter of the It's A Wonderful Life Museum. He was a true George Bailey to everyone in our community.

Small actions can have big consequences. We see it in George, and I've seen it personally in what Mr. Case did for his community.

In my soon-to-be released book *Wonderful: The Diary of George Bailey*, I imagine that on his fifth birthday young George tells his mom that he wants Lincoln Logs as a birthday gift so he can build things. Already at age five he knows what he wants to do with his life. He constructs miniatures of the bridges and buildings he dreams about. Working tirelessly on Bailey Park—a housing development to help low-income families find low-cost housing—encourages George that he is on the right path to achieving his life's goal. He shows the town he has great ideas and can see them through. He knows he can build bigger projects if only he can get out of Bedford Falls. His persistence is a good lesson for all of us: Keep going and don't give up. You've gotta follow your dream!

(Incidentally, *Follow That Dream* is the title of a good Elvis Presley movie and the name of its title song. For that same movie, Elvis recorded a song titled "What a Wonderful Life," featuring the lyric "It may go straight, or it may detour, but one thing that I know for sure, it's a wonderful life." It's the same message as in Capra's movie.)

I costarred with Elvis and lifelong friend Shelley Fabares in two movies for MGM: Girl Happy *and* Spinout. *He was a great guy, very down to earth.*

SCENE 12

That's My Business. Building and Loan.

We make a living by what we get, but we make a life by what we give.

—WINSTON CHURCHILL

INT. GEORGE'S OFFICE - DAY

CLOSE SHOT - GEORGE AND VIOLET

George has just finished writing something, and is slipping the paper into an envelope.

              GEORGE
         (hands it to her)
    Here you are.

              VIOLET
         (bitterly)
    Character? If I had any character,
    I'd . . .

              GEORGE
    It takes a lot of character to leave your
    home town and start all over again.

He pulls some money from his pocket, and offers it to her.

              VIOLET
    No, George, don't . . .

              GEORGE
    Here, now, you're broke, aren't you?

THAT'S MY BUSINESS. BUILDING AND LOAN.

> VIOLET
> I know, but . . .
>
> GEORGE
> What do you want to do, hock your furs, and that hat? Want to walk to New York? You know, they charge for meals and rent up there just the same as they do in Bedford Falls.
>
> VIOLET
> (taking money)
> Yeah - sure . . .
>
> GEORGE
> It's a loan. That's my business. Building and Loan. Besides, you'll get a job. Good luck to you.

She looks at him, then says a strange thing.

> VIOLET
> I'm glad I know you, George Bailey.

She reaches up and kisses him on the cheek, leaving lipstick. George opens the door for her.

George Bailey had helped a lot of people, and in this interaction with Violet, who is down on her luck, George likely doesn't think he is doing anything special. In the end, Violet doesn't end up needing to go to New York to look for a job. In fact, George's generosity helps change Violet's life.

Capra drives this theme home over and over again—that one seemingly small action can make a difference.

This is one of the reasons so many of us love the movie and keep coming back to its message: "You are important. You can change lives for the better. George made a difference even when he didn't realize it. And so can you." You might have already—you just don't know it! Try to make it a conscious effort.

All kinds of people step into our lives. We are impacted by more people and in more ways than we could ever realize. And conversely, we have an impact in more people's lives than we could ever begin to know. Sometimes we minimize or shortchange our influence in the world. But we may never know how someone else is touched by a kind word or deed.

Your caring smile at a passing car from the street might make the day special for that person. Perhaps you leave something extra for your server at a restaurant. You have no idea what big consequences these small acts might have in those people's lives.

So many times, these actions—whether given or received—go unnoticed or unacknowledged, but they're still life-changing.

The people who pray for us when we don't even know we are being prayed for . . .

Folks who give gifts anonymously . . .

Strangers who extend a kindness at just the moment we needed it . . .

THAT'S MY BUSINESS. BUILDING AND LOAN.

Have you ever had someone come up to you and ask, "Do you remember me?" before describing how you made a difference in their life? You might not remember what they're talking about (or you might not even know who they are!).

This happened to me. I was invited by the USO Hollywood Oversees Committee to entertain the troops in Vietnam. I had two choices: I could do a handshake-tour or a show. Songs, comedy, and, of course, *girls*. I decided to do a show, as a little competition for Bob Hope. Ha! I didn't have to go, but I was taught that you have to give back. (And you do!)

The USO advertises my performance.

THE HEART OF IT'S A WONDERFUL LIFE

I have such vivid memories of that USO tour. We were there for twenty-two days in August and September 1968. In putting the show together, I invited a good buddy of mine, Nino Candido. He brought the big laughs. Very funny on- and offstage. Nino was also a great guitarist. Nino and I had met many years earlier while doing *The Adventures of Ozzie and Harriet* TV series.

Then I was lucky to find two talented girls to join the show. One had been a finalist as a *Playboy* magazine centerfold (Jeanne Barrett), and the other was a popular actress (Salli Sachse). Salli had been in a number of beach-party films before moving on to more dramatic roles. Jeanne and Salli were no prima donnas, just dedicated and talented girls, committed to helping lift the troops' spirits. And that they did. After the forty-five-minute show, we'd walk among the soldiers to talk and answer their questions.

A young soldier came up to me after one show and said he

Nino Candido, Jeanne Barrett, Salli Sachse, and me in Vietnam.

THAT'S MY BUSINESS. BUILDING AND LOAN.

had seen me and my trick horse Pixie (from my years on the *Annie Oakley* series) when we visited Shriners Children's Hospital in Spokane, Washington, in 1957. Whenever we weren't filming, we would hit the road to appear at state and county fairs, rodeos, and home shows all over the country. We'd always make it a priority to visit the local children's hospital. Those kids couldn't get to the show, so we went to them.

This young soldier couldn't have been more than nineteen years old. He said he was one of the many kids in the hospital at that time and wanted me to know that he appreciated me and Pixie.

"You and Pixie did all your tricks, and Pixie even guessed how old I was. It was great. You were there for about an hour. And in that time none of us kids were sick," he said. "We had no pain. Our thoughts were with you and Pixie. Thank you, Mr. Hawkins."

I couldn't have been more surprised by this coincidence or honored that this young man was so encouraged by those moments years earlier.

"And thanks for coming over here too," he said. Then with a smile he continued, "And thanks for bringing the girls."

"Yeah?" I said. "Better than Pixie, huh?"

We both laughed.

Again, the theme of the movie keeps echoing. "Each man's life touches so many other lives." You just never know . . .

Don't forget! We are all important. And we can make a difference.

SCENE 13

Where's the Money?

It is a painful thing to look at your own trouble and know that you yourself and no one else has made it.

—SOPHOCLES

INT. UNCLE BILLY'S LIVING ROOM

CLOSE SHOT

A shabby, old-fashioned, gas-lit room which has been turned almost inside out and upside down in an effort to locate the missing money. Drawers of an old secretary have been pulled out and are on the floor. Every conceivable place which might have been used by Uncle Billy to put the money has been searched. George, his hair rumpled, is feverishly pursuing the search. Uncle Billy is seated behind the desk, his head on his hands.

          GEORGE
And did you put the envelope in your pocket?

        UNCLE BILLY
Yeah . . . yeah . . . maybe . . . maybe . . .

          GEORGE
          (shouts)
Maybe - maybe! I don't want any maybe. Uncle Billy, we've got to find that money!

WHERE'S THE MONEY?

> **UNCLE BILLY**
> (piteously)
> I'm no good to you, George. I . . .

> **GEORGE**
> Listen to me. Do you have any secret hiding place here in the house? Someplace you could have put it? Someplace to hide the money?

> **UNCLE BILLY**
> (exhausted)
> I've been over the whole house, even in rooms that have been locked ever since I lost Laura.

Uncle Billy starts sobbing hysterically. George grabs him by the lapels and shakes him.

> **GEORGE**
> (harshly)
> Listen to me! Listen to me! Think! Think!

> **UNCLE BILLY**
> (sobbing)
> I can't think any more, George. I can't think any more. It hurts . . .

George jerks him to his feet and shakes him. Uncle Billy stands before him like a frisked criminal, all his pockets hanging out, empty. George's eyes and manner are almost maniacal.

> GEORGE
> (screaming at him)
> Where's that money, you stupid, silly old fool? Where's the money? Do you realize what this means? It means bankruptcy and scandal, and prison!
>
> He throws Uncle Billy down into his chair, and still shouts at him:
>
> GEORGE (CONT'D)
> That's what it means! One of us is going to jail! Well, it's not going to be me!
>
> George turns and heads for the door, kicking viciously at a waste basket on the floor as he goes. Uncle Billy remains sobbing at the table, his head in his arms.

This scene is the beginning of George's unraveling.

In truth, George is ultimately responsible for the missing money. He knew Uncle Billy was dealing with memory loss—you know, the string on his fingers—but entrusted him with the deposit anyway. As the person in charge, George should have given Uncle Billy other duties that wouldn't have put the business in jeopardy.

And George's initial response—and his frustration with Uncle Billy—seems like he's going to pass the buck. "I'm not taking responsibility for this! One of us is going to jail!"

George's reaction is understandable, of course. He's under a lot of pressure. And the consequences of losing that deposit (close to $100,000 in today's money) would be devastating for George and his family and for the community.

Whether you're the head of a family or in charge at the office, you can't go around pointing the finger at someone else when mistakes happen. You have to take ownership. Perhaps you've worked for a boss who did this—took credit for the good things but then passed the buck when something went wrong. It's no way to lead.

A poem often credited to Charles Osgood, known for his work in radio and television in the 1970s to 1990s, has been condensed over the years into this brief paragraph that you've likely read before:

> There was an important job to be done and Everybody was sure that Somebody would do it. Anybody could have done it, but Nobody did it. Somebody got angry about that because it was Everybody's job. Everybody thought Anybody could do it, but Nobody realized that Everybody couldn't do it. It ended up that Everybody blamed Somebody when Nobody did what Anybody could have.

Have you experienced this before? Which "body" were you? We've all been there, and George Bailey was no different. Thank goodness he realized his error in blaming Uncle Billy and stepped up to take responsibility.

SCENE 14

What's the Matter with Daddy?

When you feel like giving up, remember why you started!

—UNKNOWN

INT. LIVING ROOM - NIGHT

CLOSE SHOT

Janie is still pounding with grim determination at the piano. Pete is seated at the table writing. Tommy is playing with his toy vacuum cleaner. The telephone rings.

              JANIE AND PETE
  Telephone.

INT. LIVING ROOM - NIGHT

CLOSE SHOT

Mary comes in and picks up the phone.

              MARY
  I'll get it.
        (on phone)
  Hello. Yes, this is Mrs. Bailey.

George enters shot, and stands listening to her.

MARY (CONT'D)
Oh, thank you, Mrs. Welch. I'm sure she'll be all right. The doctor says that she ought to be out of bed in time to have her Christmas dinner.

GEORGE
Is that Zuzu's teacher?

MARY
(hand over receiver)
Yes.

GEORGE
Let me speak to her.

He snatches the phone from Mary.

GEORGE (CONT'D)
(on phone)
Hello. Hello, Mrs. Welch? This is George Bailey. I'm Zuzu's father. Say, what kind of a teacher are you anyway? What do you mean sending her home like that, half-naked? Do you realize she'll probably end up with pneumonia on account of you?

MARY
(shocked)
George!

She puts a restraining hand on his arm. He shakes it off. She cannot know that George's tirade against Mrs. Welch is really a tirade against the world, against life itself, against God. Over the phone we hear Mrs. Welch's voice sputtering with protest.

>   GEORGE
> Is this the sort of thing we pay taxes for - to have teachers like you? Silly, stupid, careless people who send our kids home without any clothes on? You know, maybe my kids aren't the best-dressed kids; maybe they don't have any decent clothes . . .

Mary succeeds in wresting the phone from George's hand.

> GEORGE (CONT'D)
> Aw, that stupid . . .

Mary speaks quickly into the phone.

> MARY
> Hello, Mrs. Welch. I want to apologize . . . hello . . . hello . . .
> (to George)
> She's hung up.

> GEORGE
> (savagely)
> I'll hang her up!

But the telephone is suddenly alive with a powerful male voice calling:

WHAT'S THE MATTER WITH DADDY?

                    MR. WELCH'S VOICE
            Now, who do you think you are?

George hears this and grabs the receiver
from Mary.

                         GEORGE
                       (to Mary)
            Wait a minute.
                       (on phone)
            Hello? Who is this? Oh, Mr. Welch?
            Okay, that's fine, Mr. Welch. Gives me
            a chance to tell you what I really
            think of your wife.

Mary once more tries to take the phone
from him.

                         MARY
            George . . .

                         GEORGE
                     (raving at her)
            Will you get out and let me handle
            this?
                    (into phone - shouting)
            Hello? Hello? What? Oh, you will,
            huh? Okay, Mr. Welch, any time you
            think you're man enough . . . Hello?
            Any . . .

But before he can think of an insult to
top Welch's, we hear a click on the phone.

> GEORGE

Oh . . .

He hangs up the receiver, and turns toward the living room. His face is flushed and wet.

> PETE

Daddy, how do you spell "Hallelujah"?

> GEORGE
> (shouts)

How should I know? What do you think I am, a dictionary?

He yells at Tommy, noisily playing with his vacuum cleaner.

> GEORGE

Tommy, stop that! Stop it!

Janie is still practicing at the piano, monotonously.

> GEORGE
> (savagely)

Janie, haven't you learned that silly tune yet? You've played it over and over again. Now stop it! Stop it!

INT. LIVING ROOM - NIGHT

CLOSE SHOT

The room has suddenly become ominously quiet, the only SOUND being George's labored breathing. George goes over to a corner of the room where his workshop is set up - a drawing table, several models of modern buildings, bridges, etc. Savagely he kicks over the models, picks up some books and hurls them into the corner. Mary and the children watch, horrified. George looks around and sees them staring at him as if he were some unknown wild animal. The three children are crying.

> **GEORGE**
> (gasping for breath)
> I'm sorry, Mary, Janie. I'm sorry. I didn't mean . . . you go on and practice. Pete, I owe you an apology, too. I'm sorry. What do you want to know?

> **PETE**
> (holding back his tears)
> Nothing, Daddy.

Mary and the children stare at him, stunned by his furious outburst. There is silence in the room.

> **GEORGE**
> What's the matter with everybody? Janie, go on. I told you to practice.
> (shouts)
> Now, go on, play!

Mary and the children are shaken by George's outbursts.

Janie breaks into sobs.

                JANIE
Oh, Daddy . . .

                MARY
      (in an outburst)
George, why must you torture the children? Why don't you . . .

The sight of Mary and the children suffering is too much for George.

                GEORGE
Mary . . .

> He looks around him, then quickly goes
> out the front door of the house. Mary
> goes to the phone, picks it up.
>
>   MARY
> Bedford, two-four-seven, please.
>
>   PETE
> Is Daddy in trouble?
>
>   JANIE
> Shall I pray for him?
>
>   MARY
> Yes, Janie, pray very hard.
>
>   TOMMY
> Me, too?
>
>   MARY
> You too, Tommy.
>   (on phone)
> Hello, Uncle Billy?

Jimmy Stewart actually scared us kids when we filmed this master scene.

When we did the long shots on the stage, Capra filmed it all—except for the close-ups of us kids reacting. They brought us back in later along with another director, Slavko Vorkapich, to get the close-ups.

When he was hired to do the montage scenes, he had asked

THE HEART OF IT'S A WONDERFUL LIFE

to be second unit director if one was needed. He was important enough in capturing montages that Capra made that a part of his deal.

So, true to his word, Capra had Vorkapich direct our close-ups during the George meltdown.

I remember him very well. After setting up the lighting, Mr. Vorkapich called for me to come in. He never yelled, "Roll 'em!" It was all done very quietly. As the camera rolled, he would explain what was going on. He would talk to me about my daddy going crazy and kicking everything over: "He's yelling and scaring you." The camera kept rolling for many minutes until he got me to go through all these emotions. When I started to tear up, Mr. Vorkapich said, "Cut!" I guess he got what he wanted. He then moved on to the next kid's close-up.

Me "reacting" to George's anger, as coached by second unit director Slavko Vorkapich.

WHAT'S THE MATTER WITH DADDY?

Next time you watch the movie, now you'll know that the close-ups on us kids in that scene were filmed days later by another director.

George is so disappointed in himself. His fuse was short. His emotions boiled over.

All those times he looked the other way...

...when his dad died and everything changed in an instant.

...when he gave his college money to Harry.

...when his brother came home from college married and unable to take over the Building and Loan like they had planned.

George had allowed himself to be put upon. In so many ways, he had turned the other cheek and forsaken his own hopes and dreams. And it had all built up to this moment when Uncle Billy lost the deposit money.

And on this night, it bursts out in a destructive way—against his own family.

His anger is really directed toward himself—but the children don't know that. They only know that their father is scaring them. In his frustration, George kicks over and destroys the models he has built, all those miniature dreams he had been hanging on to for years. He breaks the very things that he had placed so much meaning in. His emotions are uncontrollable. George storms out of the house in shame with a profound sense of despair and the belief his life is worthless.

We are destined to experience both times of celebration and times of disappointment.

But we don't have to live permanently in that pain when things don't go our way. Yes, disappointment hurts. But the way we respond to it long term is in our hands. The event itself isn't what should mark our experience. Our response is what either leaves us in a state of pain ... or encourages us to learn and grow and move forward. And many times, with wisdom and hindsight, those disappointments or setbacks can end up being blessings.

SCENE 15

You're Worth More Dead Than Alive

Each man's life touches so many other lives. When he isn't around, he leaves an awful hole, doesn't he?

—CLARENCE

WIPE TO:

INT. POTTER'S OFFICE IN BANK - NIGHT

MEDIUM CLOSEUP

Potter is seated at his desk, his goon beside him. He is signing some papers. George is seated in a chair before the desk, without a hat or coat, covered lightly with snow. . . .

              GEORGE
            (desperate)
Please help me, Mr. Potter. Help me, won't you please? Can't you see what it means to my family? I'll pay you any sort of a bonus on the loan . . . any interest. If you still want the Building and Loan, why I . . .

              POTTER
           (interrupting)
George, could it possibly be there's a slight discrepancy in the books?

GEORGE
No, sir. There's nothing wrong with the books. I've just misplaced eight thousand dollars. I can't find it anywhere.

POTTER
(looking up)
You misplaced eight thousand dollars?

GEORGE
Yes, sir.

POTTER
Have you notified the police?

GEORGE
No, sir. I didn't want the publicity. Harry's homecoming tomorrow . . .

POTTER
(snorts)
They're going to believe that one. What've you been doing, George? Playing the market with the company's money?

GEORGE
No, sir. No, sir. I haven't.

POTTER
What is it - a woman, then? You know, it's all over town that you've been giving money to Violet Bick.

GEORGE
(incredulous)
What?

POTTER
Not that it makes any difference to me, but why did you come to me? Why don't you go to Sam Wainwright and ask him for the money?

GEORGE
I can't get hold of him. He's in Europe.

POTTER
Well, what about all your other friends?

GEORGE
They don't have that kind of money, Mr. Potter. You know that. You're the only one in town that can help me.

POTTER
I see. I've suddenly become quite important. What kind of security would I have, George? Have you got any stocks?

GEORGE
(shaking his head)
No, sir.

POTTER
Bonds? Real estate? Collateral of any kind?

YOU'RE WORTH MORE DEAD THAN ALIVE

GEORGE
(pulls out policy)
I have some life insurance, a fifteen thousand dollar policy.

POTTER
Yes . . . how much is your equity in it?

GEORGE
Five hundred dollars.

POTTER
(sarcastically)
Look at you. You used to be so cocky! You were going to go out and conquer the world! You once called me a warped, frustrated old man. What are you but a warped, frustrated young man? A miserable little clerk crawling in here on your hands and knees and begging for help. No securities - no stocks - no bonds - nothing but a miserable little five hundred dollar equity in a life insurance policy. You're worth more dead than alive. Why don't you go to the riff-raff you love so much and ask them to let you have eight thousand dollars? You know why? Because they'd run you out of town on a rail . . . But I'll tell you what I'm going to do for you, George. Since the state examiner is still here, as a stockholder of the Building and Loan, I'm going to swear out a warrant for your arrest. Misappropriation of funds - manipulation - malfeasance . . .

THE HEART OF IT'S A WONDERFUL LIFE

>   George turns and starts out of the office
>   as Potter picks up the phone and dials.
>
>   POTTER (CONT'D)
>   All right, George, go ahead. You can't
>   hide in a little town like this.
>
>   George is out of the door by now.
>
>   **CAMERA MOVES CLOSER to Potter.**
>
>   POTTER (CONT'D)
>   (on phone)
>   Bill? This is Potter.

Up to this point, most of us would say that life is going pretty well for George. He has a beautiful wife, four children, and a lot of friends. Despite having to set aside some of his dreams, he has even pursued building a community with affordable homes in Bedford Falls.

When he leaves Potter's office in this scene, George is feeling a mix of despair, frustration, and a deep sense of betrayal. He realizes with clarity that Potter, who represents greed and thinks only of himself, has no intention of helping him or the Building and Loan. This stark realization only magnifies George's feeling of being trapped in a difficult situation he cannot escape. In his mind, there is no way out, especially considering his worries for the community and for Bailey Brothers Building and Loan.

YOU'RE WORTH MORE DEAD THAN ALIVE

From here, George spirals downward. He has negative thoughts and feels empty and guilty. When George becomes overwhelmed at the ramifications of all the money he can't repay, he realizes that maybe Potter has hit the nail on the head:

"I'm worth more dead than alive."

In that moment, all George can see is the dark side of his life. He has lost sight of the many blessings he still has—or that there could possibly be a good outcome. In a moment of despair, it is so easy to forget all the goodness in our lives.

The element of possible suicide in this movie sparked conversation then and still does today. Govan A. Martin III, executive director and founder of the Suicide Prevention Alliance, shared in a letter to me the impact the movie has had on attitudes toward suicide in American culture. Here is a portion of it:

> In 1946, Frank Capra put together a movie that was fraught with the reality of life: that life was *not easy* and was very complicated. One of the themes of the movie that has been talked about more in recent years is the aspect of suicide. In 1946, 16,152 people in the United States died by suicide. At that time, suicide was looked at purely as a mental illness. Suicide was also looked at as a sin and a crime. *It's a Wonderful Life* has saved many lives from suicide with its key themes of hope, community, and the impact of how individual lives can impact one another.
>
> In 1974, a clerical error let *It's a Wonderful Life* come into

the public domain and then began its life on television. Fans grew exponentially year after year during the holidays, watching this classic movie. As more people watched and dissected this movie, the discussion of suicide started to come up more and more.

In 1987, a Florida judge ordered a man to watch the film as part of his sentence for killing his wife and then trying to kill himself. According to the judge, he wanted to show the man the value of life. That same year, former National Security Advisor Robert C. McFarlane told a *New York Times* interviewer that after watching the movie he could identify with George Bailey and understood the importance of each person and their role in humanity.

Some mental health professionals have credited *It's a Wonderful Life* as being a form of cognitive and behavioral therapy for those suffering, as it encourages the viewer to refocus on the positives—family, love, and friendship—just as Clarence did with George.

It's a Wonderful Life is in the zeitgeist of not only the holidays, but each day of the year, and with that, the prevention of suicide is so much more in the forefront. Suicide prevention is talked about more now than ever. There is also an interesting correlation—with the increased popularity of *It's a Wonderful Life*, the discussion about suicide continues to grow as well. There is finally a real discussion between mental health professionals and those who have lived experience of suicide (attempt survivors of suicide, loss survivors who have lost loved ones to suicide, and those currently having thoughts of suicide). Those with lived experience are more comfortable talking openly about how the movie has impacted them and what mental health professionals can do to help those who currently think about suicide.

The underlying theme of *It's a Wonderful Life* was the topic of suicide, but now with the millions of people that it has helped, the movie has created the optimism of real hope and the many ways to get help.

I had a wonderful friend—very giving with a good heart and soul. He worked for years for one of the biggest stars on the planet. He left this star to pursue his own dreams. He moved back to Memphis to start a new career. He found somebody to share his life with, but unfortunately, it didn't work out. When you are in love, you don't always think straight. Ultimately, he took his own life.

From time to time, I kick myself, thinking, *Why didn't he call me? I know I could have talked this out with him. We've all been dumped by someone, maybe even more than once. But you get over it and move on. There will always be another streetcar coming along.* But he didn't see it that way. I kept thinking I'd be able to say just the right words. Like, *Come on, how many times have I called, complaining about relationships? You talked to me and assuaged my feelings, and I moved on.* I would have repeated those words

THE HEART OF IT'S A WONDERFUL LIFE

back to him. We could have talked and listened to each other for hours, and eventually he could have moved on.

I know I could have helped—or at least, I would have tried, if only he had reached out.

As I have mentioned, *It's a Wonderful Life* received mixed reviews and was ultimately unsuccessful at the box office. At the time, the country was looking for an upbeat and uplifting story without all the drama and angst of the movie's themes, let alone an underlying theme of suicide. The movie was in and out of the theaters by early 1947.

Despite this, there was no shortage of interest. Capra received more than fifteen hundred letters from San Quentin prison soon after the movie debuted about how the film impacted inmates. They saw the message of getting a second chance. The same

A program announcing a showing of It's a Wonderful Life *at Attica Correctional Facility in New York.*

response came in 2018, when I brought the movie to Attica Correctional Facility. Those inmates sent letters about how inspired they were by the film. Over the years, Capra received many letters about this theme, and he answered every one of them.

Frank Capra's movie and the character of George Bailey tell us that we can all find the strength to persevere through the many obstacles of life, especially with friends and family surrounding us. This movie reminds us that life is worth living.

SCENE 16

"I'm Not a Praying Man, But . . ."

If we don't know how or what to pray, it doesn't matter. He does our praying in and for us, making prayer out of our wordless sighs.

—ROMANS 8:26 MSG

INT. MARTINI'S BAR - NIGHT

CLOSE SHOT

The place is an Italian restaurant with bar. The bottles sparkle. There are Christmas greens and holly decorating the place. It has a warm, welcoming spirit, like Martini himself, who is welcoming new arrivals. The booths and the checkered-cloth-covered tables are full. There is an air of festivity and friendliness, and more like a party than a public drinking place. George is seated at the bar - he has had a great deal to drink, far more than he's accustomed to. . . .

CAMERA MOVES CLOSER to George. Nick, the bartender, is watching him solicitously. Seated on the other side of George is a burly individual, drinking a glass of beer. George is mumbling:

> GEORGE
> God . . . God . . . Dear Father in Heaven, I'm not a praying man, but if you're up there and you can hear me, show me the way. I'm at the end of my rope. Show me the way, God. . . .

"I'M NOT A PRAYING MAN, BUT . . ."

George has repeatedly stood up to Old Man Potter, refusing to buckle under the pressure to sell the Building and Loan or accept a job from the town bully. Right now, he's a broken man. He'll try anything now—even prayer.

See how George Bailey prays? This is good prayer!

The way George asks God for help is so moving and sincere. If God doesn't help George, George doesn't have another option. This is it. He needs God's help. And there is power in prayer!

George says that he isn't a praying man. That line is such a comfort for so many of us who at various times may feel like we don't have the words to pray. The good news is that God doesn't need us to have the right words. When we come to Him with the same kind of spirit George has—begging for His help, sincere, humble—God is listening and ready to help.

George Bailey did the best he could for as long as he could. But circumstances eventually became too much. He was out of options—at least options that relied on his abilities.

Standing on that bridge, George prays again.

I was a kid during World War II, and one phrase was repeated often: "There are no atheists in foxholes." In times of extreme fear or desperation, as in war, even committed atheists will reach out to a higher power. When we have hit bottom, we may feel there is only one way out. And George felt that too.

Jimmy Stewart's heartfelt performance here is often considered a highlight of the movie.

During filming, when the scene was over, Capra knew that

he wanted to push in closer with the camera to punch up the importance and raw emotion of what Stewart was bringing to the scene. Capra asked Stewart if he could do it again.

Stewart said no. And Capra understood.

He knew Jimmy had gone somewhere dark to achieve that performance and didn't want to force him to relive it for another take. So Capra reshot the scene in postproduction, mechanically moving in slowly, closer and closer, on the original take, to capture the soul of this moment through George Bailey's eyes and visible emotion. Stewart later recalled, "As I said those words . . . I felt the loneliness, the hopelessness of people who had nowhere to turn, and my eyes filled with tears. I broke down sobbing. That was not planned at all."

The film—and the audience—are richer for Stewart's honest and nuanced performance.

```
INT. TOLL HOUSE ON BRIDGE - NIGHT

MEDIUM SHOT - GEORGE, CLARENCE,
AND THE TOLLKEEPER

                    GEORGE
          I found it out a little late. I'm worth
          more dead than alive.
```

"I'M NOT A PRAYING MAN, BUT..."

Clarence and George in the tollhouse, shortly after meeting.

CLARENCE

Now look, you mustn't talk like that. I won't get my wings with that attitude. You just don't know all that you've done. If it hadn't been for you . . .

GEORGE
(interrupts)
Yeah, if it hadn't been for me, everybody'd be a lot better off. My wife, and my kids and my friends.
(annoyed with Clarence)
Look, little fellow, go off and haunt somebody else, will you?

CLARENCE

No, you don't understand. I've got my job . . .

GEORGE
(savagely)
Aw, shut up, will you.

Clarence is not getting far with George. He glances up, paces across the room, thoughtfully.

CLARENCE
(to himself)
Hmmm, this isn't going to be so easy.
(to George)
So you still think killing yourself would make everyone feel happier, eh?

GEORGE
(dejectedly)
Oh, I don't know. I guess you're right. I suppose it would have been better if I'd never been born at all.

CLARENCE
What'd you say?

GEORGE
I said I wish I'd never been born.

CLARENCE
Oh, you mustn't say things like that. You . . .
(gets an idea)
. . . wait a minute. Wait a minute. That's an idea.
(glances up toward Heaven)

"I'M NOT A PRAYING MAN, BUT..."

```
What do you think? Yeah, that'll do it.
All right.
          (to George)
You've got your wish. You've never been
born.
```

In granting George's wish never to be born, Clarence believes George will discover he wants people to respect him and realize his life is valued. Like George, we all encounter struggle and hardship. Sometimes life is frustrating. Sometimes we fail. Sometimes we might even reach the end of our rope and wonder, *Is this all there is?*

George didn't recognize his life's purpose until he bottomed out and ended up questioning his very existence.

SCENE 17

You Really Had a Wonderful Life. Don't You See?

To the world you may be one person, but to one person you may be the world.

—DR. SEUSS

EXT. STREET - NIGHT

MEDIUM SHOT - GEORGE MOVES INTO THE SCENE

The sign bearing the name of the town reads: "Pottersville." George looks at it in surprise, then starts up the street toward the main part of town. As he goes, CAMERA MOVES WITH him. The character of the place has completely changed. Where before it was a quiet, orderly small town, it has now become in nature like a frontier village. We see a SERIES OF SHOTS of night clubs, cafes, bars, liquor stores, pool halls and the like, with blaring jazz MUSIC issuing from the majority of them. The motion picture theatre has become a burlesque house. Gower's drugstore is now a pawnbroker's establishment, and so on.

CLOSE SHOT

George stops before what used to be the offices of the Building and Loan. There is a garish electric sign over the entrance reading: "Welcome Jitterbugs." A crowd of people are watching the police, who are raiding the place, and dragging out a number of screaming women, whom they throw into a patrol wagon. George talks to one of the cops:

> GEORGE
> Hey . . . hey. Where did the Building and Loan move to?

> COP
> The Building and what?

> GEORGE
> The Bailey Building and Loan. It was up there.

> COP
> They went out of business years ago.

MEDIUM CLOSEUP

George sees the struggling figure of Violet Bick, arrayed as a tart, being dragged into the patrol wagon. . . .

EXT. BAILEY HOME - NIGHT

MEDIUM SHOT

George runs up the path to the front door of the house and raps on the door. He rings the bell and taps on the glass, when his attention is caught by a sign on the wall reading: "Ma Bailey's Boarding House."

MED CLOSEUP - GEORGE AT THE DOOR

The door opens and a woman appears. It is Mrs. Bailey, but she has changed amazingly. Her face is harsh and tired. In her eyes, once kindly and understanding, there is now cold suspicion. She gives no sign that she knows him.

>   MA BAILEY
> Well?

>   GEORGE
> Mother . . .

>   MA BAILEY
> Mother? What do you want?

It is a cruel blow to George.

>   GEORGE
> Mother, this is George. I thought sure you'd remember me.

>   MA BAILEY
>   (coldly)
> George who? If you're looking for a room there's no vacancy.

She starts to close the door, but George stops her.

>   GEORGE
> Oh, Mother, Mother, please help me. Something terrible's happened to me.

I don't know what it is. Something's happened to everybody. Please let me come in. Keep me here until I get over it.

MA BAILEY
Get over what? I don't take in strangers unless they're sent here by somebody I know.

GEORGE
(desperate)
Well, I know everybody you know. Your brother-in-law, Uncle Billy.

MA BAILEY
(suspiciously)
You know him?

GEORGE
Well, sure I do.

MA BAILEY
When'd you see him last?

GEORGE
Today, over at the house.

MA BAILEY
That's a lie. He's been in the insane asylum ever since he lost his business. And if you ask me, that's where you belong.

She slams the door shut in George's face.

EXT. HOUSE - NIGHT

MEDIUM CLOSE SHOT

George stands a moment, stunned. Then he turns and runs out to the sidewalk, until his face fills the screen. His features are distorted by the emotional chaos within him.

George is devastated that his mother doesn't recognize him.

The role of George Bailey ran the gamut for an actor—great highs and terrible lows. But as any actor can attest, many of us try to dig down in our memory bank for personal experiences we might bring to the character.

Mr. Stewart had drawn upon different experiences in his life and captured those emotions on-screen in the past. But the role of George Bailey brought with it depth that Jimmy Stewart hadn't explored.

I learned that after George and Mary's wedding scene, the newlyweds were supposed to drive away in George's car. So as not to hang things up, Stewart went to Capra and explained he didn't want to do all that driving, especially in downtown traffic and on the way to the train station. He told Capra he was afraid he'd get into an accident. Apparently this kind of reaction was because of what he was suffering after the war. Capra started to question him but noticed right away that Stewart was getting edgy. He told Stewart he understood and would take care of it. So he rewrote the scene as if George's pal Ernie was taking the wedding couple in his cab to the depot to catch the train for their honeymoon.

Capra was seeing in Stewart what he saw in other returning veterans: His experience in the war had changed him. To play George Bailey, Stewart would need to mine for some deep and raw emotions, which wasn't difficult given that those feelings were at the surface already. It's highly likely those life-altering war experiences formed his emotional response.

At first Stewart played some of this emotion as confused. But as the scenes escalated, more and more was coming through in his performance. He really revealed those emotions in the scene where he leaves his mother's house. Capra had him run off the porch to a very big close-up—the entire screen actually.

You could see the fright in Stewart's eyes in that scene.

Long after the release of *It's a Wonderful Life*, it was reported that Jimmy Stewart had come home after WWII with a serious health issue: what is now known as PTSD, or post-traumatic stress disorder. In 1946 they called it "shell shock" or "combat fatigue." He was deeply affected by his time in the service:

> "I tried with all my might to lead and protect them," he said of his Airmen. "I lost a few men—all my efforts, all my prayers couldn't stand between them and their fates, and I grieved over them, blamed myself, even. But my father said something wonderful to me when I came home after the war. He said, 'Shed all blame, shed all guilt, Jim. You know you did your very best, and God and fate, both of which are beyond any human being's efforts, took care of the rest.'"

Stewart came home a changed man. His parents were upset by how much he had aged. He was thinner; his face looked tighter. The press asked about his gray hair. He said: "It got pretty rough overseas at times."

And Stewart brought that pain to *It's a Wonderful Life*: "His anger in the film is raw, edgy, breaking the confines of the sentimental story."

```
EXT. HOUSE - NIGHT

We see Clarence leaning on the mail box
at the curb, holding his volume of "Tom
Sawyer" in his hand.
```

> YOU REALLY HAD A WONDERFUL LIFE. DON'T YOU SEE?

> CLARENCE

Strange, isn't it? Each man's life touches so many other lives, and when he isn't around he leaves an awful hole, doesn't he?

> GEORGE
> (quietly, trying to use logic)

I've heard of things like this. You've got me in some kind of a spell, or something. Well, I'm going to get out of it. I'll get out of it. I know how, too. I . . . the last man I talked to before all this stuff started happening to me was Martini.

> CLARENCE

You know where he lives?

> GEORGE

Sure I know where he lives. He lives in Bailey Park.

They walk out of scene.

WIPE TO:

EXT. CEMETERY - NIGHT

MEDIUM SHOT

George and Clarence approach the tree from which the "Bailey Park" sign once hung. Now it is just outside a cemetery, with graves where the houses used to be.

CLARENCE
Are you sure this is Bailey Park?

                    GEORGE
Oh, I'm not sure of anything anymore.
All I know is this should be Bailey
Park. But where are the houses?

The two walk into the cemetery.

                    CLARENCE
              (as they go)
You weren't here to build them.

CLOSE MOVING SHOT

George wandering like a lost soul among
the tombstones, Clarence trotting at his
heels. Again George stops to stare with
frightened eyes at:

CLOSE SHOT - A TOMBSTONE

Upon it is engraved a name, Harry Bailey.
Feverishly George scrapes away the snow
covering the rest of the inscription, and
we read: "IN MEMORY OF OUR BELOVED SON -
HARRY BAILEY - 1911-1919"

CLOSE SHOT - GEORGE AND CLARENCE

                    CLARENCE
Your brother, Harry Bailey, broke
through the ice and was drowned at the
age of nine.

George jumps up.

> **GEORGE**
> That's a lie! Harry Bailey went to war! He got the Congressional Medal of Honor! He saved the lives of every man on that transport.

> **CLARENCE**
> (sadly)
> Every man on that transport died. Harry wasn't there to save them because you weren't there to save Harry. You see, George, you really had a wonderful life. Don't you see what a mistake it would be to throw it away?

CLOSEUP - GEORGE AND CLARENCE

> **GEORGE**
> Clarence . . .

> **CLARENCE**
> Yes, George?

> **GEORGE**
> Where's Mary? . . .

WIPE TO:

EXT. LIBRARY - NIGHT

CLOSE SHOT

Mary comes out the door, then turns and

locks it. We see George watching her from
the sidewalk. Mary is very different -
no buoyancy in her walk, none of Mary's
abandon and love of life. Glasses, no
make-up, lips compressed, elbows close to
body. She looks flat and dried up, and
extremely self-satisfied and efficient.

CLOSEUP

George, as he watches her.

CLOSE SHOT

George and Mary, on the sidewalk.

>   GEORGE

Mary!

She looks up, surprised, but, not
recognizing him, continues on.

>   GEORGE (CONT'D)

Mary!

Mary starts to run away from him, and he
follows, desperately.

>   GEORGE (CONT'D)

Mary! Mary!

He catches up to her, grabs her by the
arms, and keeps a tight grip on her. She
struggles to free herself.

Mary doesn't recognize George either.

GEORGE (CONT'D)
Mary, it's George! Don't you know me?
What's happened to us? . . .

MARY
(struggling)
I don't know you! Let me go!

GEORGE
Mary, please! Oh, don't do this to me.
Please, Mary, help me. Where's our
kids? I need you, Mary! Help me, Mary!

Mary breaks away from him, and dashes
into the first door she comes to, the Blue
Moon Bar.

As we watch George stumble through the world where he doesn't exist, we can't help but begin asking ourselves, *What would life look like if I had never been born?*

THE HEART OF IT'S A WONDERFUL LIFE

The streets George is walking with Clarence are unrecognizable.

The town is now called Pottersville. No more Bedford Falls.

Where Bailey Brothers Building and Loan should have been are instead bars, clubs, and pawnshops.

George's mother has no idea who he is.

Uncle Billy is in an insane asylum.

What was Bailey Park is a cemetery.

Harry is dead . . . and so are all the men he would have saved had he made it to fight in the war.

And most painful, Mary has no memory of George. In fact, she is scared of him.

(Incidentally, years after its release, I attended a screening of the film at the Motion Picture Academy, along with Frank Capra. We got to talking, and I asked him, "If you could change anything in the movie, what would it be?" He said, without hesitation, he would have made Mary Hatch a more take-charge kind of woman, because someone who was so single-minded about pursuing George Bailey would never have turned out to be a meek librarian. She would have been a real estate broker or the owner of her own business, like a dress shop. Someone who made things happen—a real progressive woman.)

In those moments in Pottersville, George realizes the profound impact of his life—of his actions and the purpose of his life—by witnessing the bleak, corrupt reality of what his town would be without him. George has helped create community and hope. He has created opportunity for his uncle and a beautiful, loving home with Mary. His individual actions have had ripple effects.

But where is George to turn? If only he could get back!

SCENE 18

"I Want to Live Again"

Consider thyself to be dead, and to have completed thy life up to the present time; and live according to nature the remainder which is allowed thee.

—MARCUS AURELIUS, *MEDITATIONS* 7.56

WIPE TO:

EXT. BRIDGE OVER RIVER - NIGHT

MEDIUM SHOT

The same part of the bridge where George was standing before Clarence jumped in. The wind is blowing as it has all through this sequence. George comes running into shot. He is frantically looking for Clarence.

GEORGE
Clarence! Clarence! Help me, Clarence. Get me back. Get me back. I don't care what happens to me. Only get me back to my wife and kids. Help me, Clarence, please! Please! I want to live again!

CLOSEUP

George leaning on the bridge railing, praying.

GEORGE
I want to live again. I want to live again. Please, God, let me live again.

―――――――――― "I WANT TO LIVE AGAIN" ――――――――――

George sobs. Suddenly, toward the end of
the above, the wind dies down. A soft,
gentle snow begins to fall.

CLOSE SHOT - GEORGE SOBBING AT THE RAILING

The police car pulls up on the roadway
behind him, and Bert comes into scene.

                    BERT
Hey, George! George! You all right?

George backs away and gets set to hit
Bert again.

               BERT (CONT'D)
Hey, what's the matter?

                 GEORGE
                (warningly)
Now get out of here, Bert, or I'll hit
you again! Get out!

                    BERT
What the Sam Hill you yelling for,
George?

                 GEORGE
Don't . . . George?

George talks hopefully - George touches
Bert unbelievingly - George's mouth is
bleeding again.

> **GEORGE (CONT'D)**
> Bert, do you know me?

> **BERT**
> Know you? Are you kiddin'? I've been looking all over town trying to find you. I saw your car piled into that tree down there, and I thought maybe . . . Hey, your mouth's bleeding; are you sure you're all right?

> **GEORGE (CONT'D)**
> What did . . .

George touches his lips with his tongue, wipes his mouth with his hand, laughs happily. His rapture knows no bounds.

> **GEORGE (CONT'D)**
> (joyously)
> My mouth's bleeding, Bert! My mouth's bleed . . .
> (feeling in watch pocket)
> Zuzu's petals! Zuzu's . . . they're . . . they're here, Bert! What do you know about that? Merry Christmas!

He practically embraces the astonished Bert, then runs at top speed toward town.

LONG SHOT

"I WANT TO LIVE AGAIN"

George, thrilled to be alive again, races to his family.

```
George runs away from camera
yelling . . .
```

                              GEORGE

    Mary! Mary!

After what George has seen in a world where he doesn't exist, he wants his life back! And Clarence grants it. George runs joyously through the streets, yelling, "Merry Christmas!" to everybody he sees. He cannot wait to be reunited with his family.

If, like George Bailey, we could see what life would be like if we hadn't been born, I suspect we'd realize how truly fortunate we are just to be in this world. We would discover that every experience in our life, no matter how dull or how difficult, somehow is leading us to our life's purpose.

The barriers that forced George to sacrifice his dreams and instead serve the community where he grew up were, in reality, the building blocks to a life of *real* meaning. No amount of personal or business failure, of adversity, struggle, or confusion can change the immeasurable value of our lives and the difference we are already making on our journeys.

In one of my talks with Mr. Stewart, this is what he shared with me: During filming, he had doubts about whether acting and movies were actually important. He talked with Lionel Barrymore, who played Mr. Potter, about it, and that conversation really helped lift his spirits. Barrymore reminded Stewart that acting is important. Millions of people, sitting in the dark for two hours, watch you, and it helps shape their lives. Your acting has that kind of influence.

But Stewart pressed Barrymore. "Is acting really a decent vocation?"

Barrymore came right back at him and asked, "Is it more decent to drop a bomb on people than bring a ray of sunshine to them through your acting?"

He was right. Stewart had been given a great gift.

"I WANT TO LIVE AGAIN"

That's how he could relate to George Bailey. Jimmy Stewart took his own doubts and gave them to his George character.

Donna Reed had doubts too. She told Shelley Fabares during our *The Donna Reed Show* years that when she read the script and saw that Capra had her doing things she'd never done before—dancing, singing, and comedy—she was fearful.

With Donna Reed and Shelley Fabares on the very first episode of The Donna Reed Show. *Eight years later I was still being asked back.*

"My character went from a teenager to a woman of forty. None of these things I felt I could do. I was so frightened, I wanted out of the movie. In fact, I wanted out of show business. But I was under contract, and ultimately it was a very good lesson learned."

The things that frighten us most are often the very things we must do!

Just imagine if Jimmy Stewart or Donna Reed had succumbed to their fears or doubts and hadn't done this film. What a loss that would have been for all of us. And what a reminder that whatever our small (or big) role in life might be, there is purpose in it if we just keep our eyes and hearts open.

SCENE 19

No Man Is a Failure Who Has Friends

You meet people who forget you. You forget people you meet. But sometimes you meet people you can't forget—those are your friends.

—UNKNOWN

INT. LIVING ROOM - NIGHT

CLOSE SHOT

Mary leads George, who is carrying a couple of the kids on his back, to a position in front of the Christmas tree.

                    MARY
     Come on in here now. Now, you stand right
     over here, by the tree. Right there, and
     don't move, don't move. I hear 'em now,
     George, it's a miracle! It's a miracle!

She runs toward front door and flings it open. Ad lib SOUNDS of an excited crowd can be heard. Uncle Billy, face flushed, covered with snow, and carrying a clothes basket filled with money, bursts in. He is followed by Ernie, and about twenty more townspeople.

                    MARY
     Come in, Uncle Billy! Everybody! In here!

Uncle Billy, Mary, and the crowd come into the living room. A table stands in front of George. George picks up Zuzu to protect

NO MAN IS A FAILURE WHO HAS FRIENDS

her from the mob. Uncle Billy dumps the basketful of money out onto the table - the money overflows and falls all over.

UNCLE BILLY
Isn't it wonderful?

The rest of the crowd all greet George with greetings and smiles. Each one comes forward with money. In their pockets, in shoe boxes, in coffee pots. Money pours onto the table - pennies, dimes, quarters, dollar bills - small money, but lots of it. Mrs. Bailey and Mrs. Hatch push toward George. More people come in. The place becomes a bedlam. Shouts of "Gangway - gangway" as a new bunch comes in and pours out its money. Mary stands next to George, watching him. George stands there overcome and speechless as he holds Zuzu. As he sees the familiar faces, he gives them sick grins. Tears course down his face. His lips frame their names as he greets them.

UNCLE BILLY
(emotionally at the breaking point)
Mary did it, George! Mary did it! She told a few people you were in trouble and they scattered all over town collecting money. They didn't ask any questions - just said: "If George is in trouble - count on me." You never saw anything like it.

Tom comes in, digging in his purse as he comes.

>TOM
>What is this, George? Another run on the bank?

Charlie adds his money to the pile.

>CHARLIE
>Here you are, George. Merry Christmas.

Ernie is trying to get some system into the chaos.

>ERNIE
>The line forms on the right.

Mr. Martini comes in bearing a mixing bowl overflowing with cash.

>ERNIE
>Mr. Martini! Merry Christmas! Step right up here.

Martini dumps his money on the table.

>MARTINI
>I busted the juke-box, too!

Mr. Gower enters with a large glass jar jammed full of notes.

ERNIE

Mr. Gower!

GOWER
(to George)
I made the rounds of my charge accounts.

Violet Bick arrives, and takes out the money George had given her for her trip to New York.

GEORGE

Violet Bick!

VIOLET

I'm not going to go, George. I changed my mind.

Annie, the colored maid, enters, digging money out of a long black stocking.

ANNIE

I've been saving this money for a divorce, if ever I get a husband.

Mr. Partridge, the high school principal, is the next donor.

PARTRIDGE

There you are, George. I got the faculty all up out of bed.
(hands his watch to Zuzu)
And here's something for you to play with.

THE HEART OF IT'S A WONDERFUL LIFE

>   MAN
>   (giving money)
>   I wouldn't have a roof over my head if
>   it wasn't for you, George.

Ernie is reading a telegram he has just received.

A behind-the-scenes glimpse of George and the Bailey children celebrating with friends and family.

>   ERNIE
>   Just a minute. Quiet, everybody. Quiet
>   - quiet. Now, this is from London.
>   (reading)
>   Mr. Gower cables you need cash. Stop.
>   My office instructed to advance you
>   up to twenty-five thousand dollars.
>   Stop. Hee-haw and Merry Christmas. Sam
>   Wainwright.

The crowd breaks into a cheer as Ernie drops the telegram on top of the pile of money on the table.

> MARY
> (calling out)
> Mr. Martini. How about some wine?

As various members of the family bring out a punch bowl and glasses, Janie sits down at the piano and strikes a chord. She starts playing "Hark! The Herald Angels Sing," and the entire crowd joins in the singing. We see a SERIES OF SHOTS of the various groups singing the hymn, and some people are still coming in and dropping their money on the table. Carter, the bank examiner, makes a donation; the sheriff sheepishly looks at George and tears his warrant in small pieces. In the midst of this scene, Harry, in Naval uniform, enters, accompanied by Bert, the cop.

> HARRY
> Hello, George, how are you?

> GEORGE
> Harry . . . Harry . . .

> HARRY
> (as he sees the money)
> Mary - looks like I got here too late.

                    BERT
Mary, I got him here from the airport
as quickly as I could. The fool flew
all the way up here in a blizzard.

Mrs. Bailey enters scene.

                MRS. BAILEY
Harry, how about your banquet in New
York?

                   HARRY
Oh, I left right in the middle of it as
soon as I got Mary's telegram.

Ernie hands Harry a glass of wine.

                   HARRY
Good idea, Ernie. A toast . . . to my
big brother, George. The richest man in
town!

Harry Bailey toasts his brother.

Once more the crowd breaks into cheering and applause. Janie at the piano and Bert on his accordion start playing "Auld Lang syne," and everyone joins in.

CLOSE SHOT

George, still holding Zuzu in his arms, glances down at the pile of money on the table. His eye catches something on top of the pile, and he reaches down for it. It is Clarence's copy of "Tom Sawyer." George opens it and finds an inscription written in it: "Dear George, remember no man is a failure who has friends. Thanks for the wings, Love Clarence."

      MARY
    (looking at book)
What's that?

      GEORGE
That's a Christmas present from a very dear friend of mine.

At this moment, perhaps because of the jostling of some of the people on the other side of the tree, a little silver bell on the Christmas tree swings to and fro with a silvery tinkle. Zuzu closes the cover of the book, and points to the bell.

> ZUZU
> Look, Daddy. Teacher says, every time a bell rings an angel gets his wings.
>
> GEORGE
> (smiling)
> That's right, that's right.
>
> He looks up toward the ceiling and winks.
>
> GEORGE (CONT'D)
> Attaboy, Clarence.
>
> The voices of the people singing swell into a final crescendo for the
>
> FADE OUT

To George's shock, when he returns to Bedford Falls, he sees how his community has rallied around him. They have raised money and come together in prayer to support this man who has always supported them. George can't believe his eyes.

Friends are everything. But to have a friend, you must be a friend.

Friendship is more important than money or possessions. People helping other people is a tremendous source of strength and support. Be kind and serve others. You can't go wrong when you're doing right. Finding the balance between self-fulfillment and dedication to others is a major developmental task and is a continuing challenge for us all.

That emotion we experience in the final scene of *It's a Wonderful Life* is something I don't think any other film has replicated. For eighty years now, audiences have been brought to tears as George realizes how much his life is worth.

And that message is for you too. You may have faced numerous hardships. Perhaps you feel you've failed—yourself or others. Maybe you had to defer your dreams or feel they'll never come true. Perhaps you're standing at the edge of a bridge and wondering why you were even born.

Close your eyes for a moment. Look back on some of the defining moments in your life. Now envision those moments as if you'd never existed. How would the world be different? How would the people you love be different? How would your community be different?

Wouldn't it be nice if each of us could learn, as George did, that *life is already wonderful*—right now, today? That where we put our focus determines if it is so?

I receive cards and letters from people in many walks of life, even some from inmates in correctional facilities. When they watch the movie and see George's story, they come to understand the reason for their lives too. "If I hadn't been around," they say, "my aunt or uncle, brother or sister, wouldn't have done this or that."

And it's not just the fictional character of George Bailey who provides valuable lessons. The film's star, Jimmy Stewart, lived an inspiring and meaningful life as well.

In addition to his film career, Mr. Stewart signed up to fight in WWII against his studio's wishes, and he took that responsibility seriously. He flew many missions over Germany in a B-24 and retired from the US Air Force as a brigadier general. He insisted that his *It's a Wonderful Life* contract include a line ensuring that "his military exploits not be publicized."

Stewart was known as gentle and soft-spoken. He was a good businessman and very successful, but he remained humble and devoted to his faith, and he maintained a good reputation in Hollywood despite his great success. His Oscar for the 1940 movie *The Philadelphia Story* reportedly stood in his father's hardware store for years. He also received an honorary Lifetime Achievement Oscar in 1995.

Stewart was a lifelong Boy Scout, a loving father, and a devoted husband to his wife, Gloria, for more than forty-five years. Stewart was raised Presbyterian and remained devout throughout his life.

Jimmy Stewart and George Bailey had roots of character. Those who preserve their integrity remain unshaken by the storms of daily life. They do not stir like leaves on a tree or follow the herd where it runs. This is not something that is given to them by others; it is a strength that exists deep within them.

After President Harry S. Truman saw *It's a Wonderful Life*, he said, "If Bess and I had a son, we'd want him to be just like Jimmy Stewart."

Having lost Gloria to cancer several years earlier, Stewart reached the end of his life in 1997, at eighty-nine years old. His final years without Gloria had been different, and he seemed at peace with what was coming. Stewart's last words were reportedly about his beloved wife: "I'm going to be with Gloria now."

What a glorious ending to his wonderful life!

CONCLUSION

After All Is Said and Done

Take peace! The gloom of the world is but a shadow. Behind it, yet within reach, is joy. There is a radiance and glory in the darkness, could we but see. And to see, we have only to look. I beseech you to look!

—FRA GIOVANNI (THIS WAS FRANK CAPRA'S FAVORITE QUOTE)

When *It's a Wonderful Life* was released, audiences were concerned about the movie's ending. Many felt Capra had left the elephant in the room unaddressed—what happened to Old Man Potter?

Why didn't he get his comeuppance? Why didn't we see him punished? Everyone knows that the bad guy always gets it in the end! And we don't get to see that as *It's a Wonderful Life* draws to a close.

I asked Mr. Capra that very question at an Academy of Motion Picture Arts and Sciences event called "Director's Choice." Academy members (I was invited to become a member in 1961) and students of cinema and theater were invited to attend these screenings—with the director available for discussion and question. Mr. Capra, of course, was there to screen and discuss *It's a Wonderful Life*.

So why didn't Potter experience consequences at the end of the movie?

Here's what Mr. Capra told me:

How do you deal with this guy like [Potter]? You leave him alone. He was a go-about-his-business kind of guy who wouldn't change, couldn't change.... I was more interested in George Bailey. Potter was too crusty, too old, too happy with what he was doing. So we left him alone, let him go about his business.

No revenge, no justice in the earthly sense, just recognition that a good man, George Bailey, was in trouble and desperately needed and deserved help. The heart of the message was that redemption was available for George. Capra wanted viewers to focus on the power of good over evil rather than on a villain getting punished.

It's a message we all need to hear—over and over and over again. There may not be ultimate justice in this world, but we can depend on blessings to help us overcome obstacles and to get us through to the goodness that is available.

Capra summed it up like this: "My kind of people saw the film. And it touched their hearts and moved them to write thousands of letters, half of them first-time testimonials."

I'm so thankful that Capra never deviated from his mission for this movie. His vision was clear, and he never backed down. He often said it was the movie he was born to make—a beautiful reminder, in scene after scene, that one person can make a difference.

And that person is you!

It really is a wonderful life, isn't it?

Epilogue

It's a Wonderful Life *isn't the way life is . . .
just the way it should be!*

—FRANK CAPRA

It's a Wonderful Life stands on its own, even all these years later. There's never been another film like it, nothing as magical and heartfelt as what Capra created. People may say they've watched something that reminds them of *It's a Wonderful Life*, but I personally don't think another movie in history has come close.

I love watching people watch this movie—whether it's for the first time or the hundredth. "Lifers" settle in for that familiar feel-good buzz that they experience every time they see it or when they look at photos or read articles about it. And I catch first-timers tearing up without fail. Most of all, I love hearing people talk about the movie. It has this inarguable ability to bring people of all stripes together as we ponder what it really and truly means to have a wonderful life.

The enduring messages of faith, hope, and life renewed in *It's a Wonderful Life* remain so important today. Times can be trying, money may be tight, and holding families together sometimes feels more difficult than ever. I'm so grateful this movie lives on as a reminder to us all, as we journey along with George Bailey, of what really counts in life—the things you *can't* put a price tag on. Family, friends, and the belief in miracles.

EPILOGUE

Here's how these messages have resonated in my life: I optioned a book that took me nine years to get to the screen. I knew all along it was a great story, and I didn't give up, even though I got rejected time after time, much like Philip Van Doren Stern did. I kept dreaming I could sell it. I just had to find that one studio, network, or cable channel that would give me the green light.

I look at a project, whether it's a script, a book, a story, or a newspaper or magazine article, as a football. My job is to carry it downfield into the end zone to score. When I get the ball, I start running, looking for the light, a place I can squeak through. I don't stop until I make it past the goal line.

In your life, the ball's been given to you on whatever field you're playing on. It's up to you to make a touchdown so your dream can come true too. As I've said, don't give up; you've got to keep going. Don't let anyone or anything stop you. Go for it. Dreams come true. They have for me. Not the way I planned them, but when they came true, they were bigger and better than I could have imagined. But of course, that was God's plan.

Frank Capra had a plan: win the Oscar for Best Director and show the new filmmakers that he still had it. But that wasn't God's plan. What God had in mind was bigger and better than if *It's a Wonderful Life* had won all five Oscars it was nominated for.

It was God's plan to have the movie's copyright fall into the public domain, triggering hundreds of TV stations everywhere

EPILOGUE

to show it for free, making it one of the most popular and inspirational movies of all time. Thank God He let Capra live long enough to see it. God has a plan for each of us.

The scenes that I chose to talk about are some of my favorites. You probably have your favorites too—moments you discuss with others and how they resonate in today's culture. That's good. The baton has been passed to you to touch lives for the better.

I hope that as you've read this book, you've captured that feeling of self-worth and purpose you experienced when you first saw *It's a Wonderful Life*. And I hope it continues to instill in you and in those you love all the success, joy, and wonders you're looking for.

With great appreciation and warm regards, I wish you love, happiness, and . . . a wonderful life.

Jimmy Hawkins

Acknowledgments

I am indebted to the following institutions and individuals for their assistance and support in the preparation of this book: The Frank Capra archives at Wesleyan University, especially Jeanne Basinger; the Seneca Falls It's A Wonderful Life Museum, and Anwei and Henry Law; Ned Comstock and the USC Cinema Television Library; Bud Barnett of Cinema Collectors; Fred Capozzi; Govan Martin of the Suicide Prevention Alliance; Joe Zimmermann; and Judy Coppage.

In appreciation to copy editor Jenifer Gott.

Special thanks to Meaghan Porter, senior editor. Your notes made me dig deeper, making all the difference. Big difference. Thank you. They said you were the best.

And of course, Matt Baugher, senior vice president of HarperCollins Focus, who put *his* focus on the project, making it all happen. It's been a pleasure.

Clarence sure was right when he said, "Each man's life touches so many other lives. When he isn't around he leaves an awful hole."

Thank you all for being around. You made Little Tommy Bailey look . . . well, wonderful.

Notes

Introduction

x **Voted the most inspirational movie of all time:** "AFI's 100 Years ... 100 Cheers: The 100 Most Inspiring Films of All Time," AFI (American Film Institute), accessed March 17, 2025, https://www.afi.com/afis-100-years-100-cheers/.

xi **"I didn't give a film clip":** Frank Capra, *The Name Above the Title* (Grand Central Publishing, 1997), 383.

xiii **"a politician who rises from an idealistic state assemblyman":** Joseph McBride, *Frank Capra: The Catastrophe of Success* (University Press of Mississippi, 2011), 521.

Scene 1: Capravision

4 **Capra defied gossip columnist Hedda Hopper's reporting:** "Donna's First Role Off the MGM Lot," Donna Reed, accessed March 23, 2025, https://www.donnareed.org/post/donna-s-first-role-off-the-mgm-lot.

4 **Capra was bringing on other writers to rewrite:** McBride, *Frank Capra*, 513.

4 **"slow and pretentious":** "Walker Lenses 'Life,'" *The Hollywood Reporter*, May 21, 1946, 4.

5 **Vic was replaced by Capra's longtime cameraman:** McBride, *Frank Capra*, 528.

5 **Capra and Tiomkin weren't in sync:** Michael Willian, *The*

NOTES

Essential It's a Wonderful Life: A Scene-by-Scene Guide to the Classic Film (Chicago Review Press, 2006).

8 **grossing only $3.3 million:** Johnny Oelksinski, "Classic 'It's a Wonderful Life' Started as a Box Office Flop That Critics Dismissed: 'Embarrassing,'" December 24, 2024, *New York Post*, https://nypost.com/2024/12/24/entertainment/classic-its-a-wonderful-life-started-as-a-box-office-flop-that-critics-dismissed-embarrassing/.

8 **"The weakness of this picture":** "'It's a Wonderful Life' (1946) Review," archived from Bosley Crowther, "'It's a Wonderful Life', Screen in Review," December 23, 1946, *The New York Times*, December 11, 2018, https://www.nytimes.com/2018/12/11/movies/its-a-wonderful-life-review.html.

8 **"so mincing as to border on baby talk":** John McCarten, "The Current Cinema," *The New Yorker*, December 21, 1946, 87.

9 **"It is not the critic who counts":** Theodore Roosevelt, "The Man in the Arena," *Citizenship in the Republic*, speech delivered at the Sorbonne, April 23, 1910, https://www.theodorerooseveltcenter.org/Learn-About-TR/TR-Encyclopedia/Culture-and-Society/Man-in-the-Arena.aspx.

Scene 3: The Hero Inside of You

19 **"A person who saves one soul":** Eliyahu Touger (translator), "Mishneh Torah, The Sanhedrin and the Penalties within Their Jurisdiction," Sefaria.org, accessed March 23, 2025, https://www.sefaria.org/Mishneh_Torah%2C_The_Sanhedrin_and_the_Penalties_within_Their_Jurisdiction.12.3?lang=bi.

19 **"a person admired":** *Merriam-Webster*, s.v. "hero," accessed May 21, 2025, https://www.merriam-webster.com/dictionary/hero.

NOTES

22 **"What is a hero?":** Jonathan Limehouse, "Trailer for Christopher Reeve 'Super/Man' Documentary Offers Glimpse into Late Actor's Life," *USA Today*, August 26, 2024, https://www.usatoday.com/story/entertainment/movies/2024/08/26/superman-christopher-reeve-documentary/74951987007/.

Scene 10: A Run on the Bank

77 **Building and Loans slowed foreclosures:** John Wake, "What 'It's a Wonderful Life' Shows Us About the Weird History of Building & Loans," *Forbes*, December 31, 2021, https://www.forbes.com/sites/johnwake/2021/12/31/its-a-wonderful-life-and-the-weird-history-of-building—loans/.

Scene 15: You're Worth More Dead Than Alive

117 **"In 1946, Frank Capra put together a movie":** Letter from Govan A. Martin III, executive director and founder of the Suicide Prevention Alliance, to the author.

120 **Capra received more than fifteen hundred letters from San Quentin prison:** Patrick Coffin, "*It's a Wonderful Life*: The Little Story That Did," *National Review*, December 24, 2012, https://www.nationalreview.com/2012/12/its-wonderful-life-little-story-did-patrick-coffin/ (accessed March 20, 2025).

Scene 16: "I'm Not a Praying Man, But . . ."

126 **"As I said those words":** Howard Mansfield, "Heroes and Leaders: Jimmy Stewart," *Air & Space Forces*, March 28, 2024, https://www.airandspaceforces.com/article/heroes-and-leaders-jimmy-stewart/.

NOTES

SCENE 17: YOU REALLY HAD A WONDERFUL LIFE. DON'T YOU SEE?

138 **Jimmy Stewart came home after WWII with a serious health issue:** Dan Bates, "How Jimmy Stewart's Agony in It's a Wonderful Life Came from Extreme PTSD He Suffered After He Lost 130 of His Men as Fighter Pilot in WWII," *Daily Mail*, October 6, 2016, https://www.dailymail.co.uk/news/article-3825552/Jimmy-Stewart-suffered-extreme-PTSD-lost-130-men-fighter-pilot-WW-II-acted-anguish-filming-s-Wonderful-Life.html.

137 **"shell shock" or "combat fatigue":** Nina Metz, "How Jimmy Stewart's War Service Affected 'It's a Wonderful Life,'" *Chicago Tribune*, June 19, 2018, https://www.chicagotribune.com/2016/11/30/how-jimmy-stewarts-war-service-affected-its-a-wonderful-life/.

138 **"I tried with all my might to lead and protect them":** Mansfield, "Heroes and Leaders: Jimmy Stewart."

138 **"His anger in the film is raw":** Mansfield, "Heroes and Leaders: Jimmy Stewart."

SCENE 19: NO MAN IS A FAILURE WHO HAS FRIENDS

166 **"his military exploits not be publicized":** "James Stewart, the Hesitant Hero, Dies at 89," *The New York Times*, July 3, 1996, https://www.nytimes.com/1997/07/03/movies/james-stewart-the-hesitant-hero-dies-at-89.html.

167 **"If Bess and I had a son":** "James Stewart, the Hesitant Hero."

CONCLUSION

170 **How do you deal with this guy like [Potter]?:** From a personal conversation with the author in his audiobook, *Wonderful Memories of It's a Wonderful Life* (Blackstone Audio, 2005).

About the Author

Jimmy Hawkins portrayed the son of some of Hollywood's most popular movie stars of the 1940s, such as Spencer Tracy, Katharine Hepburn, Greer Garson, Lana Turner, and Jessica Tandy. Jimmy also has the distinction of playing Jimmy Stewart and Donna Reed's son, Tommy Bailey, in the Frank Capra film classic *It's a Wonderful Life*. He worked with Mr. Stewart on two other films: Cecil B. DeMille's *Greatest Show on Earth* and Universal's *Winchester 73*.

Jimmy was reunited with Donna Reed when he was signed to play Mary Stone's (Shelley Fabares) boyfriend, George/Scotty, for eight seasons on *The Donna Reed Show* on ABC from 1958 to 1966. He costarred as Elvis Presley's sidekick in two MGM musicals, *Girl Happy* and *Spinout*. He appeared in over forty movies and three hundred-plus TV shows.

Jimmy turned to producing in 1969. Along with many other credits as producer, he produced the all-star television special for PBS based on the Lux radio version of *It's a Wonderful Life*

ABOUT THE AUTHOR

in celebration of its fiftieth anniversary. He is currently developing a major motion picture on the life of Dr. Mary Walker, the only woman in history to be awarded the Congressional Medal of Honor.

All of Jimmy's producing credits have a similar theme. The stories are rich in color but above all deal with simple honesty, plain decency, and old-fashioned values that point to the eventual betterment of the human spirit.

Jimmy is the author of five popular *It's a Wonderful Life* books and served on the advisory boards of the Jimmy Stewart Museum, the Donna Reed Foundation, and the Seneca Falls It's a Wonderful Life Museum.

He's involved in various charitable organizations, and in 1968 he was invited by the USO Shows and the Hollywood Overseas Committee to entertain the troops in Vietnam.

Jimmy is celebrating over sixty years as a member of the Academy of Motion Picture Arts and Sciences.